Cesar Millan's
LESSONS FROM
THE PACK

Also by Cesar Millan

Cesar Millan's
Short Guide to a Happy Dog

Cesar Millan's
LESSONS FROM THE PACK

Stories of the Dogs Who Changed My Life

Cesar Millan
With Melissa Jo Peltier

NATIONAL GEOGRAPHIC
Washington, D.C.

Published by National Geographic Partners
1145 17th Street NW Washington, DC 20036

Some names and identifying details have been changed in order to protect the privacy of individuals and organizations.

ISBN: 978-1-4262-1613-8 (hardcover)
ISBN: 978-1-4262-1618-3 (export edition)

Since 1888, the National Geographic Society has funded more than 12,000 research, exploration, and preservation projects around the world. National Geographic Partners distributes a portion of the funds it receives from your purchase to National Geographic Society to support programs including the conservation of animals and their habitats.

National Geographic Partners
1145 17th Street NW
Washington, DC 20036-4688 USA

Become a member of National Geographic and activate your benefits today at natgeo.com/jointoday.

For information about special discounts for bulk purchases, please contact National Geographic Books Special Sales: specialsales@natgeo.com

For rights or permissions inquiries, please contact National Geographic Books Subsidiary Rights: bookrights@natgeo.com

Interior design: Nicole Miller

Printed in the United States of America

16/QGF-LSCML/1

To honor the spirit of dogs, in gratitude for everything they have done for me and my family, I dedicate this book to my soulful canine teacher, Daddy. He believed in himself, he believed in me, and he taught me how to help others. Daddy, please keep guiding me to be as wise and good as you were. It was my great privilege to walk beside you, my friend. Everybody misses you—especially me.

God gave unto the Animals
A wisdom past our power to see:
Each knows innately how to live,
Which we must learn laboriously.

—Margaret Atwood,
"God Gave Unto the Animals"

Contents

Animals enter our lives prepared to teach and far from being burdened with an inability to speak, they have many different ways to communicate. It is up to us to listen more than hear, to look into more than past.

—Nick Trout,
Love Is the Best Medicine

Introduction:

Meet Your New Teachers

Close your eyes with me. Just for a moment. Close your eyes and imagine a day like this:

The morning birds are chattering outside the window as you awaken naturally at dawn—you don't need an alarm clock to tell you when to start your day. The moment the sunlight hits your eyes, you are filled with a mingled sense of excitement, joy, and anticipation. You go seamlessly into your morning yoga routine, stretching and loosening up every muscle in your body before you hurry outside for your morning exercise.

Walking through your neighborhood and reveling in your good health, you take every possible moment to breathe in the fresh air, the scent of the flowers, grass, and trees all around you. Though this is the same walk you take every day, you appreciate it all as if you're experiencing it for the very first time. You see your friends and neighbors, and you linger to greet them enthusiastically, as they, in return, greet you. They, too, are excited about the day that lies ahead.

When you return home for breakfast, your family awaits you. You greet them with even more joy and unbounded love than you did your neighbors. You embrace them, kiss them, and let them know how much you adore and appreciate them before you all rush into the yard and playfully celebrate another day you all get to be together. This is your morning routine every day—because what is life for, if not to share this incredible sense of wonder and gratitude you feel with the ones you love the most?

When it's time to go to work, you arrive with anticipation—you love what you do for a living! It gives you a great sense of pride and self-esteem. You greet each of your colleagues warmly. Even though they are all so very different from you on the outside—different heights and weights, colors, races, religions—you share the understanding that you're all one species with one common purpose. You respect all the people you work with, from the ones with the most menial jobs to the CEO. And even the CEO shares this accepting attitude. Your company's philosophy is that everyone has a vital role to play in the work you do, and everyone should share fairly in the proceeds.

Every once in a while, you have a disagreement with someone at work. They might have something you want, or perhaps they do something that you don't agree with. But there's no backstabbing in your company—no silent plots, no whispering at the water cooler. No: When you and a colleague don't see eye-to-eye, you speak your mind right away, even if it means a short dustup between the two of you. It'll be over within minutes, the matter will be decided, and you'll go on with your day without rancor or resentment.

Sounds like a perfect world, doesn't it? And probably an impossible one—more like an urban fairy tale.

But not necessarily. The scenario I just outlined is a snapshot of what life could be like if humans approached life the way dogs do.

Dogs show us the best we can be.

Over the past 10 years, I've written six books on the subject of canine behavior, nearly all of them *New York Times* bestsellers. All contain stories of the many dogs I've rehabilitated over the years and the techniques I've used to help them. In those books, I was the teacher. But this book is very different. In this book, the dogs are not the students; they are the teachers. Our teachers. In the pages that follow, I will share for the first time some of the most important lessons that the dogs in my life have taught me.

Our dogs are right in front of us every day, showing us with their every action a better way to live. All too often, we don't pay attention. We take them for granted, thinking we know so much more about life than they do and believing that we have far more to teach them than they could possibly teach us.

In fact, we invest an enormous amount of energy trying to get our dogs to become more like us! We teach them to understand our language—often without even bothering to learn theirs. We teach them to sit, stay, come, and heel for our convenience, not theirs. We pamper them like children (when they really don't care about who has the prettiest toys), and we dress them in couture outfits (when they couldn't give a hoot about fashion).

None of that makes sense to me. Here we are teaching our dogs to behave as we do even while many of us struggle to find happy relationships with members of our own species. Dogs are designed by nature to value qualities like honor, respect, ritual, compassion, honesty, trust, loyalty, and compassion. They instinctually understand the importance of pack hierarchy and mutually beneficial relationships. So instead of teaching them what we think they should learn from us, what if we took the opportunity to learn from them?

I'm writing this book because I believe it's time that we start looking at our dogs as our teachers. Dogs have all the qualities we say we want, but we never seem to be able to attain. Every day of their lives, dogs actually live the moral code that humans only aspire to. And I believe dogs often understand us better than we understand ourselves.

Socrates said, "Know thyself." I have my own variation on that adage: If you want to know yourself, know your dog! After all, in a way, your dog knows you—the real you—better than most people in your life do. Your dog knows your routines. Your dog understands how to read your body language and your emotions—probably far better than you do yourself. Your dog reveals your hidden subconscious thoughts and is a mirror of your deepest soul.

No philosophers so thoroughly comprehend us
as dogs and horses.
—Herman Melville

The Evolution of a Teacher

Dogs have become our best teachers because, out of necessity, they have been diligent students of human behavior for centuries. Through millennia of evolution, they have learned to study our species to be able to successfully live alongside and cooperate with us.

Think about it: Dogs have migrated with our species over thousands upon thousands of miles. They have hunted with us; they have herded our livestock and defended our territories. They have walked beside us and adapted along with us at every stage of our journey, following us as we changed from hunter-gatherers to farmers to industrialized city dwellers.

Over these many years, dogs have come to know our habits almost as well as they know their own. They've learned to read our body postures and to understand our vocal nuances. In order to survive, they've become the world's foremost experts on every type of human behavior. I am convinced that if dogs could speak our language, they would be our best psychologists, as well as our best friends and teachers.

There are more than 400 million dogs in the world. Approximately one in every four families in the United States has a dog. It doesn't matter if you're rich or poor, religious or atheist, or if you live in a big city or on a small ranch in the country. Dogs know how to cooperate and live anywhere with any of us.

Because they are so adaptive, dogs are among the only animals that have been able to coexist happily with humans for tens of thousands of years. In their eye-opening book *The Genius of Dogs,* research scientists Brian Hare and Vanessa Woods theorize that when prehistoric wolves first began to evolve into the animal we know today, they "domesticated" humans as much as we domesticated them. They learned quickly that if they helped us hunt, herd our sheep, and protect our homes, there would be a reward for them, too: food and shelter, which eventually evolved into a unique cross-species affection.

Imagine the moment some 34,000 years ago when that first clever wolf/protodog figured out that all its life's needs would be taken care of if it simply helped this strange, upright creature do what wolves naturally did every day: hunting, scouting, tracking, and protecting their families. Wolves who did not fear or threaten humans suddenly had an advantage that their "wilder" cousins didn't have. It was a win-win situation that has continued to this day.

While our dogs have strived to understand us in order to fit into our world, we haven't always shown them the same courtesy. Most of my clients come to me thinking a dog's issues have nothing to do with them. In nearly every case, a dog's problems begin with its owners. Whatever their profession or cultural background, the people I work with all have a similar plea: "Cesar, please, please help my dog!" What I have to teach them all to understand is that before I can help their dog, they have to learn how to help themselves.

The Evolution of a Best Friend

Dogs have been by our sides, observing us and reading our energy, during every phase of our evolution. When we needed protection, they figured out how to communicate with us, to warn us of oncoming danger. When we needed transportation, they gamely agreed to pull our sleds and wagons. And when we needed companionship, they stepped up and learned how to become our best friends.

As human civilization evolved, we eventually didn't need dogs for most of the physical chores they once performed. But even today, they are still adapting to our newest dilemmas. Dogs help us detect disease, aid us in search-and-rescue missions, offer comfort therapy in hospitals, and bring companionship and cheer at home.

Our relationship with dogs has always involved a deeper connection than does our relationship with other pets like goldfish, ferrets, farm animals, or even cats. Perhaps because we are both social species, humans and dogs have a shared understanding of and appreciation for what it means to both rely on and care about others.

Over time, dogs have graduated from being our helpers to our companions to our full-fledged family members. Their deceptively simple perspective on life offers us an ideal glimpse of what trust, respect, devotion, and loyalty in relationships should look like. It makes sense that in their next evolutionary role, they should become our greatest teachers.

I think dogs are the most amazing creatures;
they give unconditional love. For me they are
the role model for being alive.
—Gilda Radner

The Most Important Lessons in Life

As a child, I learned about respect from the dogs that roamed our farm, soaking up their lessons of nonconfrontational conflict resolution and social self-awareness. I learned serenity by observing the peaceful cooperation of the pack. I

*Between home and the Dog Psychology Center, I am surrounded
by an ever growing pack of beautiful dogs.*

learned honesty and integrity by absorbing the simple and
direct way these animals communicated with each other.
Dogs were my role models, and dogs helped me become who
I am today. They continue to make me want to be a better
man: a better companion, friend, father, and teacher.

To learn from dogs, we first must connect with them—and
not from a place of superiority. We need to humble ourselves
and be open to a different kind of communication. To learn
from dogs—or from any animal, for that matter—we must first
understand their world by trying to see life through their eyes.

Our lives are so complicated these days. While we right-
fully take pride in the revolutionary technology society has
to offer, we forget that it can also lead us further and further
away from our instinctual natures. For us, stressful jobs, long
commutes, and hours spent hunched over our computers
seem normal. Our children have more homework than play-

time. They don't relax by climbing trees anymore; instead, they stay inside, glued to a pulsing video screen. We have houses to clean, errands to run, debts to settle, bills to pay. If we let ourselves get too lost in those details, we'll never have the chance to see the world and all its precious moments—the way that a dog does naturally.

Given all this, I believe that the secret to inner peace and happiness lies in the instinctual world, where dogs live 24-7. We are animals first and foremost, and we know when something doesn't feel right in our lives. So we read self-help books and self-medicate with food, drink, drugs, gambling, and shopping—all in a desperate attempt to shut out the noise and find peace. But it turns out that we have the best role models in the world living right beside us in our homes.

Dogs can teach us so many life lessons—for example, about trust, loyalty, serenity, and unconditional love. I touch on all of these in the pages that follow. But above all, I want to share with you eight specific lessons that some very special dogs in my life have taught me about respect, freedom, confidence, authenticity, forgiveness, wisdom, resilience, and acceptance. I have learned these lessons from my beloved pit bulls Daddy and Junior; from a proud and honorable farm dog named Paloma; from a couple of massive Rottweilers named Cain and Cycle; and even from a little French bulldog named Simon. So many dogs have passed through my life, but each has left an indelible mark. As you'll see, each chapter represents a concrete, inspiring step on a journey to self-discovery based on the lessons our dogs can teach us.

I've talked for many years about leaders and followers. But I think it's high time for us to "follow" dogs by adopting their worldview, their lifestyle, and their values (which are the social values of the pack). A dog lives his life unselfishly, always putting the welfare of the pack ahead of his own interests. Living in the moment, dogs do not get lost in the trees before first experiencing all the beauty of the forest.

In this moment in human history, it's imperative that we adopt this pack-oriented worldview. We need to go back to common sense, to simplicity, and to gratitude for what we have. We postpone the most important things in life: family, health, joy, and balance. Dogs do not. When they sense an imbalance—in an environment, in a situation, or in a person—they don't think about what they're going to do to fix it. They simply react, much in the same way we might recoil from touching a hot flame. And when it comes to figuring out what's going on with a human's volatile emotions, dogs are virtuosos.

If we watch them more closely and listen more carefully, our beloved pets can be the keys to our personal growth and self-knowledge. The wisdom of dogs is medicine for the soul—but in our species' self-centered world, we often forget to pay attention.

So come with me on a journey that will reveal a new way of living our lives—based on the unique and insightful lessons we can learn from our dogs.

LESSON I: RESPECT

We are sun and moon, dear friend; we are sea and land. It is not our purpose to become each other; it is to recognize each other, to learn to see the other and honor him for what he is: each the other's opposite and complement.
—Hermann Hesse, *Narcissus and Goldmund*

H e had the same appearance as the other dogs on the farm: wolf-shaped head, slightly curled tail, long legs, and a skinny coyote-like body. But you could always tell it was Paloma because of his coat: a pure, creamy white, so very different from the brown and gray coats of the rest of the pack. Even when he was backlit against the setting sun and his color wasn't easily visible, there was something else about this animal that stood out as he returned from another long, hot day in the fields. Trotting across the crest of the slope, dust from the well-trodden earth billowing with his every step, he emanated exceptional dignity.

Always following just behind or beside my grandfather, but in a position ahead of the other men and dogs, Paloma stood as proud and straight as the *pitaya* trees that dotted the hills around the state of Sinaloa, our home in Culiacán on the west coast of Mexico. His ears were pointed and alert, turning side to side like satellite dishes searching for signals. He held his head and neck erect; even while standing like a statue his eyes remained in motion, alert to everything around him.

Paloma was unmistakably the pack leader of the seven or so farm dogs that lived with us—just as my grandfather was unmistakably the leader of his own pack (which included our family, the dogs, and the day workers). But Paloma was also my grandfather's lieutenant. He may have been a different species, but there was no doubt he was second in command. The dogs and farmhands alike could sense it.

As my grandfather's right hand, Paloma was a presence to be reckoned with, respected and honored by his community. Like my grandfather, Paloma was a natural leader, calm and low-key but incontestably in charge. Like my grandfather, Paloma worked every day from dawn until dusk to earn his living. And like my grandfather, he was responsible for the safety and welfare of those in his charge.

As a very small boy living on the farm with my grandfather and grandmother, my mother and father, and my younger sister, Nora, I was fascinated by Paloma. I would observe his behavior with the other dogs: how he corrected the pups, how he kept order when a disagreement broke out, and especially how he instinctively responded to my grandfather's needs before he could even communicate them. I remember staring deep into Paloma's light brown eyes and experiencing the thrill of his looking right back at me—not just an animal but a deep, knowing soul. There was an understanding there, a timeless wisdom.

I remember a moment when Paloma spoke to me with his eyes: "One day, you'll lead a pack of your own."

FAST-FORWARD NEARLY 40 YEARS. Paloma and his pack are long gone—the curse of being human is that we will likely outlive almost all the dogs that we've ever known and loved. But as I sit here today, looking out at the rolling hills and valleys that surround my Dog Psychology Center in Santa Clarita, California, I can still picture them—not as ghosts, but as living, breathing spirits whose energy still vibrates in these hills.

Looking back, I realize that I first experienced leadership by watching my grandfather manage the farm. He didn't have to order people around like a bully. He didn't get angry or show fear when the crops were wilting from a lack of water. Because of his strong and steady hand, everyone, including the animals, willingly obeyed him.

Paloma was the equivalent of my grandfather in the animal world, inspiring the same kind of respect. He didn't have to bark or growl to get pack members to follow him. He never appeared anxious or afraid when the animals were under stress from heat or hunger.

I realize now that my grandfather and Paloma shared a trait that I would work very hard to attain later in life: the ability to encourage trust and inspire respect in others. You can't be a leader unless you've earned respect by building mutual trust, which is the cornerstone of both human and canine relationships. Leaders who fail in this regard often resort to fear-based authority—a style that doesn't work in the animal world or in the human-canine relationship.

There's a long-standing myth in my industry that I use a "dominance style" training method. The word "dominance" in reference to dogs at the head of the pack continually gets misinterpreted to mean "domination" or "intimidation." That's not the kind of leadership I learned from my grandfather and Paloma, and it's not the kind of inspirational leadership I advocate. The building blocks of pack leadership are respect and trust, not fear and domination.

The Circle of Life

I was born and passed the most formative years of my childhood on my grandfather's farm in Culiacán, Mexico. Ours was a very traditional country life. We all worked every day to keep the farm going; my grandfather, my grandmother, my father and mother, and even us kids, had our own chores and responsibilities. (At first, it was just my sister Nora and I; later my sister Monica and brother Erick arrived.)

My grandfather was a tenant farmer, which meant that although he didn't own his land, he was allowed by the property owner to live on it. Every day of his life, he got up and worked—milking cows, raising pigs for meat, collecting eggs, and harvesting vegetables. Sometimes he moonlighted as a miner. He survived by exchanging this hard labor for use of the land and the essentials he needed to take care of his family. He died on the farm at the age of 105.

This sort of existence probably sounds like a time capsule from the distant past—and in a sense, it is. But that's life in a developing country. Today members of my extended family back in Mexico still live in pretty much the same way.

When I was about six, my family and I moved to the city

*My family lived and shared the work on my grandfather's farm
in Culiacán on the west coast of Mexico.*

of Mazatlán, 125 miles away from my grandfather's ranch.
But I still spent all my summers at the ranch until I was in
my late teens. Looking back, I know I idealize this time and
even today credit those early simple days on the farm with
learning what true balance and happiness feel like.

But the reality was that life on the farm wasn't always
idyllic. Our entire family worked from dawn to dusk. There
was no room for any person or any animal that didn't pull
their own weight. We especially relied on the dogs—for
herding our goats and cattle; for protecting our crops from
scavengers like mice, rabbits, and birds; and for acting as
watchdogs, alerting us to the approach of predatory animals
and unknown humans.

My grandfather probably wouldn't have been able to keep
his landlord happy and our family fed if it hadn't been for
Paloma and his pack.

Paloma Joins the Family

On a farm in Mexico, you buy, sell, or trade your working animals—your cows, your horses, and your pigs—but your dogs are usually somehow just there. Still, the story of how Paloma came to us was a little more special.

One summer when I was a toddler, my grandfather was visiting a neighboring farm and learned that one of their dogs had just given birth to a litter of puppies. Curious, he asked to see them. One white puppy stood out among his gray and brown siblings. He was clearly the alpha: high energy, proud, nudging and nuzzling his brothers and sisters away from the mother's teat. My grandfather, who was completely attuned to the different energies of every animal, saw that the little white pup was a leader and was impressed by his strength. He asked the neighbor if he could exchange one of his pigs for the white dog when the puppy was old enough to leave his mother, and the farmer agreed.

Why my grandfather named his new puppy Paloma, the Spanish word for "dove," I never knew. In English, it sounds like a girl's name, but words in Spanish are both masculine and feminine. Maybe Paloma reminded my grandfather of a white dove.

Everyone Equal Under the Sun

On his farm, my grandfather, my father, and the other laborers worked in harmony with the animals. The animals were all part of what we were doing together. The dogs didn't live in the house; we didn't feed them kibble or give them bubble baths. But at the same time, they were our family. Imagine a group of relatives who live right next door and are totally in tune with you and your life, yet who have their own rituals, customs, and culture. That's pretty much what it was like.

The dogs even spoke our language. I'm not talking about Spanish; I'm talking about the language of energy. They were in tune. There was no discrimination, hierarchy, or ranking; we all shared a deep sense of mutual respect and a trust of all being together in the service of the same goal. There was no feeling that the chicken was worth less than the cat, that the cat was worth less than the dog, or that the dog was worth less than the horse, because each one of them served a larger purpose.

Unlike the pet owners I've worked with since I came to America, members of my family didn't say "I love you" to our animals. While Paloma was always at my grandfather's side, my grandfather never let the dog sleep in his bed or gave him treats or toys. Instead, he respected him by always showing Paloma gratitude, making sure he and his pack were fed, sheltered, and watered. In return, Paloma inspired my grandfather's respect by being consistent, reliable, and responsive to whatever his human family needed at the moment. Respect, to my mind, is its own powerful form of love.

My grandfather taught me that you always have to trust the animal; you have to respect the animal. The more you need the animal, the more respect you have to give. Think about it. If you don't have a rope to catch your lost donkey, all you can offer to inspire him to come with you is trust and respect. When you gain the trust of any animal, that trust becomes a rope, but not a rope of force. Trust is the rope of mutual cooperation.

The dog is the most faithful of animals, and would be much esteemed were it not so common. Our Lord God has made His greatest gifts the commonest.
—Martin Luther

Learning From Mistakes

When you live in a cooperative community like my grandfather's farm, making a mistake is a big deal, and the consequences can be severe. Of course, I was a little boy, and a high-energy, curious, mischievous one at that. I drove my mother crazy because I always wanted to look deeper into things; I was always asking, "Why?" Kids are bound to make missteps and test their boundaries—and believe me, I did.

One day when I was around six, I had a fight with my little sister. My mother had taken her side, which made me furious. I marched out the door in a huff, planning to run away to the fields where my father and grandfather were working.

As I stormed out of the house, I passed within two feet of our horse, which was tied up outside. He immediately sensed my anger and started to pace and kick. Then I stomped through the yard where we kept the chickens, which had been calmly pecking away. As soon as I drew near them, they also picked up on my rage and scattered nervously out of my way. The rooster squawked, flapped its wings, and chased after me. Finally, I reached the donkey, which was drinking water from a long trough by the path to the fields. The donkey was the only animal I was allowed to ride, so I jumped on his back and gave him a kick. This donkey—one of the most mellow, low-key animals you ever could meet—started to buck and nearly threw me off. Then he refused to move.

I never made it out to the fields that day. I just waited in a glum state of self-pity until I saw Paloma coming over the hill with my father and grandfather as they headed toward the house for dinner. I ran to my grandfather and told him all about how unfairly I felt I had been treated— how even the animals wouldn't let me get away from the house. My grandfather chuckled a little.

"Whether your sister did you wrong or not, it doesn't matter," he said. "But how you reacted was very wrong. You poisoned the whole farm with your anger. The animals were trying to correct you. But you weren't listening to them. You didn't respect what they were telling you about your own behavior."

My grandfather made me understand that like a rock thrown in a pond, my intention to flee and my anger created a negative ripple in the energy of the farm. Sharing that kind of destructive energy with animals breaks the bond of trust and respect that is so essential in an interconnected system. When animals don't trust you, they will try to correct you (sometimes using force), run away from you, or make you run away from them.

"Never blame the animals," my grandfather told me again and again. "If the animals are acting up, it's because of something you did. You must always respect them, because you are responsible for them."

In time, I came to understand what I'd done wrong: I'd disrespected the balance and the interdependence that kept the farm flowing smoothly. Any small mistake in a symbiotic world threatens the security of everyone in it. Of course, I was young, and I was inexperienced. But thanks to my grandfather and the animals on the farm, I quickly learned how to control my own behavior and temper.

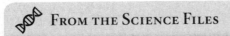

FROM THE SCIENCE FILES

In the Dog World, Respect Means Playing Fair

After years of researching dog, wolf, and coyote behavior, animal ethologist Marc Bekoff has come to believe that "playing fair" and clearly communicating intention explain why canine societies function so smoothly: Fair play and clear, honest communication are both hallmarks of mutual respect.[1]

For example, when dogs and wolves play, they instinctively try to even the playing field: A larger wolf won't bite a smaller one as hard as he could, while a dominant dog in the pack will roll over and expose her belly to a lower-status one. Both actions say, "This is all in fun—nothing serious here." Moreover, if a dog accidentally goes too far and hurts her partner in play, that dog will always "apologize" with a play bow that the other dog recognizes as "Oops! Sorry! Let's get back to the game."

By showing one another respect during play, dogs and wolves are able to keep their packs stable and their conflicts minimal. By the same token, Bekoff believes that this mutually respectful social behavior in wolves and dogs can help us better understand the roots of our own human morality—due in part to our excellent ability to cooperate with one another.

Will Work for Food

In my books and television shows, I always stress that dogs—in fact, all animals—have the inborn need to work for food and water. We humans have that need, too. As I've mentioned, everybody in my family worked, from the horses to the dogs to the humans.

But sometimes on the farm, food was scarce. On occasion my mother had to make a soup out of beans and stretch it to feed six people. If the harvest was bad, all I'd get was a tortilla and a bowl of soup to last all day. I rarely talk about my near-constant hunger. That knifelike sensation of emptiness in my belly made me angry and short-tempered, and sometimes I'd act out. Even as an adult, the feeling of hunger reminds me of that anger. I have to check myself and remember to stay in the present to avoid getting sucked into the feeling of "want" from my past.

On the farm, if we humans were hungry, the dogs were hungry, too. The chickens were content with worms, bugs, or grain; the horses, mules, and cows could eat grass. But the dogs depended on our leftover scraps—meat and beans and tortillas.

When our cupboards were bare, Paloma would lead the other dogs to scrounge whatever they could from the land. The pickings were slim. They were lucky if they caught a rabbit or fish or bird or tortoise. But unlike me, the dogs never got irritable when they were hungry. They didn't moan and whine; they didn't release their frustration on us. They went to work every day. They took care of their pups. They were totally free to come and go as they pleased, but they wanted to go to work and help us. Unlike their human counterparts, they didn't punch in late, cut corners, or take days off. The dogs all understood that they were a valued part of the farm, and that made the work joyful for them.

I was in awe of their patience, dedication, and consistency. How could you not respect that work ethic?

 ## How Dogs Show Respect

- By acknowledging and respecting proximities (meaning another animal's personal space or "territory")

- By instituting a structured, mannerly way of approaching one another

- By honoring each dog's position and abilities in their pack; from the low-energy dog at the back, to the happy-go-lucky guy in the middle, to the higher alpha in front, they understand that every position is important

- By agreeing on whether they will be following or leading

The Hierarchy of Respect

A pack of dogs has three positions—the front, the middle, and the back—and each position plays a crucial role in the pack's survival. The front dog is the leader. Like Paloma, he's curious, calm, assertive, and confident. He leads the pack not only through their daily routine but also on new and exciting adventures. The middle dog is easygoing and happy-go-lucky. She keeps up the pace for the pack. And the dog who brings up the rear is the sensitive one. He's observant, alert, and hyperaware of the environment, including any lurking potential dangers.

Because dogs don't live as long as we do, and because I'm constantly meeting and working with new canine souls, my pack these days is in flux. I like to keep my "at home" pack fairly small and manageable. Right now it consists of six dogs, most of them on the small side. The elder statesman is 14-year-old Coco, a teacup Chihuahua who grew up with my youngest son, Calvin, and shares his self-possessed, assertive personality. Despite his age, feisty Coco still rules the roost. He's been with me through many changes in my life, so we share a special bond—even though his favorite human of all time will always be Calvin. Their connection runs deep because they are truly kindred spirits. If Calvin were a dog, he'd be Coco, and vice versa.

Also at the front of the pack is Benson, a platinum-blond, beguiling Pomeranian furball. He may weigh only four and a half pounds, but Benson has a huge personality and was born to lead. He's strong, determined, confident, and a whirlwind of energy, always ready for an outdoor adventure—especially if it involves his favorite thing: water! Watching him dive and splash in my backyard pool, I think he looks more like he was born to be a porpoise than a dog.

Next, there's Junior, my muscular, athletic, gray-coated "blue" pit bull. Junior is a solid middle-of-the-pack dog: He's laid-back, happy-go-lucky, and energetic. He's not remotely interested in leading; he's happy to follow, as long as there's a whole lot of play involved. Play, play, play—to Junior, the world is one big, wonderful game, and everything in it is a toy. He doesn't really care who the winner is as long as he gets to

Here I am with part of my pack: Junior (left), Alfie (top),
Benson (center), and Taco (right).

join in. But when I need him to calm down and behave in a submissive manner, he's always happy to oblige, because he knows there will always be another game of fetch in his future.

Because of his even temperament, Junior is my right-hand guy: the dog that helps me rehabilitate unbalanced dogs, both on and off television. He is amazingly mellow and gentle, and he travels everywhere with me. In fact, Junior has the personality of that dream dog that every little girl and boy wants for a family pet: playful, obedient, and affectionate.

Alfie, a golden-blond Yorkshire terrier mix, is another middle-of-the-pack little guy. Like Junior, he is easygoing, steady, and absolutely unflappable. His mission in life is to stay either by my or my fiancée Jahira's side and go everywhere we go—which, as any dog lover knows, is the most wonderful feeling in the world. Like Junior, Alfie is the best kind of assistant you could have. He's very sensitive to the needs of all the humans and dogs around him. Some say that dogs are angels with four paws and a tail—and Alfie makes this a plausible theory. When we make eye contact and I feel him relating to me on a deep and loving level, it reminds me of how my mom looks at her children: with simple, pure, unconditional love.

Bringing up the rear of the pack is a pitch-black pug we call Gio—his name comes from the "Geo" in "National Geographic," but for fun, we gave it a distinctive spelling. Gio is the clown in the family, always making us laugh with both his purposeful and accidental antics. He can also be a bit standoffish, and his behavior seems downright catlike when it comes to cuddling with us on the couch or meeting new people. He's not fearful, but he's cautious. Gio will offer you respect and affection—but only if you earn them first.

Finally there's tiny, button-eyed Chihuahua mutt Taco, whom we rescued from the streets of Mexico. Taco is four years old but has wisdom far beyond his years. You'll sometimes find that quality in back-of-the-pack dogs; they can be shy or even a little wary of unfamiliar people and situations. But they are always acutely aware of everything going on around them and are astute observers and judges of other dogs and people. That description fits Taco perfectly.

Each day, as I watch this motley crew of dogs playing together in my backyard or at my Dog Psychology Center, I am reminded of how crucial respect is to their every interaction with one another. The leader of the pack respects the middle, and the middle respects the back, and the back respects the front, because each position offers something crucial to the others. Because of this mutual respect, there's rarely a conflict that they don't sort out quickly on their own. They are living proof of how respect occurs naturally everywhere in the animal kingdom—except, perhaps, in 21st-century humans.

Respect in the Human World

How can we be inspired to respect one another more? The answer rests in our ability to build trust. While our own species may not have done a good job of this recently, our dogs are masters at it.

I worry that, in the modern age, traditional respect is being replaced by an admiration for wealth and excess and equated with the number of "friends" or "likes" or "followers" we gather on social media. It's a sad state of affairs.

In the animal world, dogs show respect through body language. Disrespect can result in fights or becoming an outcast from the pack. In the human world, we've become so tolerant of disrespect that very often there aren't even any consequences for it. Is it any wonder that some kids today are rebellious and unstable?

The way I was raised, disrespecting a leader or an elder was unheard of; even at age 46, I'm still in the habit of calling older men and women "sir" and "ma'am." But with my own sons, Andre and Calvin, now 21 and 18, respectively, I don't sense that same kind of respect—at least not the kind that my parents and grandparents garnered. Even today, I maintain a respectful tone with my dad. Because of the nature of his role in my life, certain words will never cross my lips and I will never do certain things when I'm in his presence. That's how I was brought up.

★ FROM THE CELEBRITY FILES

The Billionaire

Too often we in the human world give our respect to the people who have power and wealth—even if they are totally unstable in their daily lives. Dogs, however, don't care what your job title is, how much money you make, or whether you have a yacht.

Take the case of "Mr. B.," one of my clients who is a well-known billionaire. Mr. B. wanted dogs for personal protection and companionship, so he bought two German shepherds from one of the best breeders and trainers in Germany.

Mr. B. called me in because he was distressed by the way one of his dogs, Max, seemed to be pulling away from him. For years Mr. B. and Max had shared a very close and loving relationship. Then suddenly Max became cold, aloof, and reluctant to share affection.

I learned that Max's first working-dog partner, Rolf, had recently died, and Mr. B. had replaced him with a new dog, Bruno. Bruno had immediately taken up the position closest to Mr. B.

I saw the problem immediately: It was simply an issue of respect. Bruno was a very dominant dog and had taken over the position of lead dog in the pack—and now occupied a status even higher than did Mr. B. himself! Max, as all dogs do, was simply showing the proper respect to his new pack leader by keeping his distance from Bruno's "property," which happened to be Mr. B.

Even though he had respect in the business world, Mr. B. didn't understand the importance of respect in the canine world. When I showed Mr. B. how to use energy and body language to reclaim his role as pack leader, Max stopped treating Bruno as his boss, and both dogs returned their respect to Mr. B. Max also resumed his formerly affectionate relationship with his owner.

To gain any dog's respect, you have to earn it. And in the dog world, respect governs behavior.

I've raised a lot of perfect dogs, but I'm still not sure how to raise a perfect child. On reflection, I sometimes feel that my ex-wife and I didn't give our boys enough rules and limitations. Of course, they grew up in a world far different from the one I did—and of course, they naturally tested their boundaries, just as I did on my grandfather's farm.

My ex-wife and I have always tried to be the best parents we could, but we often disagreed about how to raise and discipline our kids. I grew up with a very strict father—a common circumstance in Mexico. Growing up in Los Angeles, my ex was more used to the American way, where too much discipline is often seen as confining for a child's emotional development. Complicating matters was the surrounding culture, which mirrored and celebrated more lenient ways. This atmosphere is all Andre and Calvin have ever known.

The difference in our cultures and our parenting styles caused a lot of tension in our family. I'm sure we weren't alone in this. After all, kids don't come with instruction manuals, and they are certainly much harder to raise than dogs! My sons learned that they could do certain things with their mother that I would not allow. For example, I believed the boys should have regular household chores and a schedule for the weekend. As soon as they were old enough, I wanted them to hold down paying jobs so they would develop a work ethic. My ex-wife believed that the boys should enjoy the freedom of their childhood until they went away to college. For her, college was a must.

That was another point of disagreement between us: I wasn't sold on college as a necessity for them. While neither of my sons has plans to attend university in the immediate future, I would naturally be thrilled and immensely proud if they ever decide to go in that direction. All their lives, I've encouraged them to be curious, to keep learning, and to read every book they can get their hands on.

But perhaps because of my own life experience, I don't consider college itself to be a requirement for success. I believe that if you follow your passions and your instincts, they will lead you to success if you work hard; if college figures into that plan, great. Bottom line: I have always wanted the choice of whether to pursue higher education to be in my sons' own hands.

When Andre and Calvin were growing up, though, I felt that more and clearer household rules were required, along with real consequences for breaking them. My ex-wife wasn't much for punishment and instead leaned toward heart-to-heart talks and family discussions. I think that our sons became confused, and sometimes even took advantage of their parents' different philosophies in order to get their own way.

> *Intelligent dogs rarely want to please people*
> *whom they do not respect.*
> —William R. Koehler, dog trainer

Respect Others So They Will Respect You

I believe that some degree of respect and acknowledgment of roles is necessary in any group to maintain order, as is true in a dog pack. If you don't respect your parents as a young child, how can you grow up to respect your teachers? Your bosses? Your friends? Your spouse? Respect is crucial for children to learn because, just as in the animal world, it works both ways.

Pups learn respect from their mothers when they're just two weeks old. Mother dogs pick up their offspring and carry them by the nape of the neck, or nudge them with their noses when they are doing something the mother disapproves of.

I'm proud to watch my boys — now young men — growing into unique, remarkable human beings. And I'm happy to see them taking so many of the lessons I've taught them about respect to heart, now that they are able to understand them on a more mature level. When they were young teens and much more interested in impressing their peers than in listening to their parents, Andre and Calvin assumed that my work was frivolous and easy. "What our dad does on TV is stupid," they'd tell their friends, even though I knew they didn't mean it. Today, both boys have come to deeply respect what I have achieved through my television work: educating people, changing attitudes, and opening minds. It was only after developing that respect that they both became interested in how they might use the medium of television to express themselves as well.

And that interest has paid off for them. Calvin is now the star of his own Emmy-nominated children's television show, *Mutt and Stuff,* and Andre is about to launch a new television project of his own. They both carry a lot of real grown-up responsibility on their young shoulders, and they do it with aplomb. I never expected my boys would follow in my footsteps so directly, but I'm thrilled and honored to be a part of it.

Respect and Connection

Paloma taught me that respecting others is crucial to building character. In his world, species doesn't matter, nor does

*Watching Andre (right) grow into a smart, respectful young man
has reminded me of my own relationship with my father (left).*

gender, race, or creed. What matters to dogs is that everyone
does his job and honors their place in the pack.

The lesson I've learned is that when I respect the people
and dogs in my life, I show them that I am connected to
them. It's that connection that allows us to work together
to create trust: the bond that holds any pack together.

That connection also allows us to work together for the
benefit of something greater than ourselves—whether that
means putting up the family Christmas tree, sharing chores on
a farm, or collaborating with a diverse video crew for a television show. When I remember to put respect first, I feel lighter,
and all my endeavors run more smoothly and turn out better.

More than 40 years ago, a striking white-maned Mexican
farm dog named Paloma looked a curious little boy in the
eye. In that single moment of respect and connection, the

seeds of the person I have become were planted. Sometimes I think that if more people in the world had had the opportunity to learn from a teacher like Paloma, the planet would be a more cooperative, peaceful place for all of us.

Paloma's proud beauty and strong stance at the front of his pack will always epitomize for me what it means to respect and to be respected. While I am far from perfect (as my sons often remind me) and can occasionally revert back to that proud, rebellious little boy who lives inside all men, I always try to extend the same level of respect to my dogs, family, colleagues, and fans as I'd like them to extend to me. I try to remember that, symbolically, we are all working on the same "farm"—and if we live our lives with that assumption, we're much more likely to make our shared efforts a success.

 DOG LESSON #1
How to Practice Respect

- Make sure to listen. Listening creates communication and gives people the sense that they are being heard. You may not agree, but at least you are listening. That's respect.

- Always acknowledge the contribution of others, no matter how small.

- Let people be who they are. Don't judge or try to change them.

- Honor your word. Do what you say you are going to do. Honesty creates respect.

Lesson 2: Freedom

For to be free is not merely to cast off one's chains,
but to live in a way that respects and enhances
the freedom of others.
—Nelson Mandela

He was a tiny bundle of tan fur with pointy ears like a Chihuahua's, the short and scruffy body of a corgi, and warm, engaging brown eyes. His name was Regalito, and I will never forget him.

Regalito was my first pet dog. He taught me one of the most crucial life lessons I've ever learned: the necessity of freedom. From Regalito, I learned that it's vital for a dog to feel free in order to become balanced in temperament and behavior. And it's vital for every human being, too.

What is "freedom"? The word means different things to different people. When I was a 21-year-old, freedom for me was moving to another country to pursue my dreams. For someone else, it might be the freedom to leave a frustrating job or the freedom to marry whomever they want. Whatever your personal definition, you'll find that if you don't honor freedom, you cannot live a fulfilled life.

Exodus

I've mentioned that my happiest childhood memories are of my days on my grandfather's farm in Culiacán. What I don't talk about much is the period after my father decided to move us all to the city of Mazatlán, when I was around six years old. With a population of more than 400,000 people, it was to us an enormous metropolis—a place we could hardly even imagine. My parents sat me and my sister Nora down and told us that we would soon be trading the wide open spaces—vast expanses of sky, rolling green hills, and flourishing golden fields—for a small two-room apartment in a crowded two-story building.

I was heartbroken. Imagine a wild animal suddenly discovering he's being shipped off to the zoo; that's how I felt. What made it even worse was the fact that I was the reason my parents had decided to move. As the only son in my traditional, patriarchal Mexican family, I was considered the most important child. My grandfather had never gone to school, and my father had received only a third-grade education. He did not want his only boy to be ignorant or illiterate (my little brother, Erick, would not come along until I was 11). There wasn't much by way of schooling at the farm.

Watching my father pack up all our household things into my grandfather's big truck, I remember a powerful tightness in my chest. I fought to keep back the tears. What was so important about a traditional education? I was living in the best classroom on the planet—the natural world could teach me more than any school ever could! Of course, my parents didn't see it that way. My dad had already secured a very good job as a photographer and cameraman for the local news station in Mazatlán, and there was a rented apartment waiting for us. It would do me no good to whine or complain. We were definitely leaving.

The day of our departure, my grandfather saw me sulking. As I was getting into the truck, he came out of the house, carrying something in his arms. It was Regalito. Regalito means "little gift" in Spanish—an appropriate name for this dog, since it's a Mexican tradition to give gifts when people are either arriving or leaving.

Regalito was my grandfather's offering to me. He joined the group in the truck, which already held my dad's pet birds—a pair of Australian green parrots—and a few chickens my mother and sister had caged. I think in our own ways each of us wanted to keep the ranch close to us in our new life. Regalito would be the one special piece of the farm that I'd take with me.

Looking back, I don't think my grandfather was giving me the dog because he thought I'd miss the farm. I think it was his way of telling me that he would miss me. I didn't experience love in the form of physical affection until I came to America, where everybody kisses and hugs one another—even in the office! Where I came from, love was unspoken, but it could always be recognized. My grandfather's version of hugging me was gifting me Regalito as I left his house.

Some Kind of Vacation

When we first arrived in the city, my melancholy quickly turned to excitement. It was thrilling to be in the middle of so much activity. What seemed like millions of cars lined the main streets—makes and models I'd never seen before. There were stores on every block, and colorful markets crowding the alleyways with endless varieties of goods on offer. There was even a shimmering blue ocean that lapped along a golden, sandy beach—something I'd never seen before. To my young eyes, everything was new and amazing. For a little while anyway, our new life felt like a family vacation.

My dad started his new job, and I started my first day at school, where I was definitely out of my comfort zone. I hated being cooped up inside all day. My mom also had to struggle to keep the apartment in order and take care of us kids and the animals. (Think about it—she had to do all the regular housekeeping, plus clean up after the birds, the dogs, and all the chickens so that our apartment wouldn't smell bad.) At the same time, she took in sewing to earn much-needed extra income.

It turned out that Mazatlán was really expensive. At the farm, we grew and raised almost all our food, so even during the lean times my mom could always scrape together something from what we had on hand.

You couldn't do that in the city. In our small apartment—only two rooms: a combined kitchen/living area, and a bedroom—the best we could do was keep the egg-laying chickens in the already-crowded hallway. We couldn't grow our own vegetables and fruits anymore, so nearly everything we ate had to be bought at the market. Granted, the supermarket, with its abundant shelves of food, was a wonder in itself. But my parents hadn't realized how much money our lifestyle would cost. We ate a lot of cereal, tortillas, and bananas. We rarely could afford meat—a chicken or a pig's leg was a treat at Christmas. Meat was for the rich. While some people choose to eat a vegetarian diet these days, that's

I celebrated my third birthday on my grandfather's farm;
we moved to the city of Mazatlán three years later.

how my family ate all the time back then. We didn't call
ourselves "vegetarians"—we ate only vegetables because
that's all we could afford.

But it wasn't the food or the lack of money that bothered
me. It was the loss of freedom that made me feel anxious,
trapped, and constricted.

As the novelty of our new life wore off, I began to notice
all the things that I hated about the city. For one, there was
the noise: the constant clatter of vendors in the streets, the
blasting of car horns, the endless high-decibel dramas in the
neighboring apartments. The walls were tissue-thin, and
because we didn't have air-conditioning, we kept our windows open, meaning we could hear every slamming door,
every dropped plate, every shriek of joy or explosion of anger.
I missed the dark nights on the farm, where sometimes the

only sounds were the gentle songs of crickets and frogs. Many of the adults in our apartment complex would go drinking on the weekends, and they'd come home loud and acting crazy. I had never seen a drunken person before, and the sight of grown men stumbling around and mumbling strange things was really frightening.

But worst of all, instead of the city expanding my world in the way I'd first believed it would, my life seemed to be becoming smaller and smaller. There was so much crime—and right out in the open, too. We were always hearing about drugs and kidnappings, and my mother was terrified for us. She became overprotective. She set strict boundaries for where we could and couldn't go before and after school, and my parents would punish me harshly if I was caught disobeying. I disobeyed all the time. It wasn't in my nature to be fenced in.

It's better to be a free dog than a caged lion.
—Arabian proverb

Life in the Kennel

Given that I was feeling trapped, imagine what the move must have been like for Regalito. He was a little dog who had known only the freedom of the country and the constant, reassuring presence of his pack. Though his tail would wag wildly when I came home from school to play with him, or when my mother would give him a rare scrap of chicken, it was clear that he was bored and frustrated.

Regalito started exhibiting the behavior that I now know is the hallmark of an unhappy dog. He chewed the furniture and began barking all the time. He would jump at the window, desperately trying to look out. We lived on the second floor, so there wasn't much to see. To put it simply, he was living in what amounted to a kennel. And I felt like I was living in a kennel, too.

I quickly learned that, for animals, the city was a harsh place. Its residents treated dogs much less respectfully than my grandfather had. On the farm, the dogs worked side by side with us humans, as our companions and helpmates. In the city, the dogs wandered the streets in packs, stealing food and eating from garbage cans. They were considered a nuisance. People threw things at them. It was ironic—in the country, the dogs were socialized and domesticated and peaceful; but in the city, they had become almost wild again.

I'll never forget the first time I saw a dog up on a roof. This was another strange custom city people had. Most of the rooftops in Mazatlán are flat; when a stranger walks down the street in any working-class neighborhood, he'll immediately be accosted by the raucous barking of the dogs pacing the roofs high above him. That's pretty much the purpose of dogs in Mazatlán: to function as inexpensive alarm systems.

The problem is, these dogs pass their whole lives up there. They can't get down on their own, and unless a human takes pity on them, they can't go anywhere else. On the roof, they are frustrated; they pace in circles around their tiny territory, peering over the edges, growling and barking at anything out of the ordinary. Since the roof is also the place where poor families like ours would hang their laundry to dry, these dogs can become destructive. Their pent-up energy leads them to tear the clothes off the lines and chew them to pieces. Like the people in the streets, the building owners eventually come to think of them as nuisances and treat them accordingly. In Mazatlán, dogs got no respect from anyone.

For that reason, our neighbors thought we were really eccentric for keeping a dog *inside* our apartment. The chickens and parrots they could understand, but a dog? Although I was sometimes allowed to take Regalito to the beach on weekends and let him run and play around on our roof for exercise, most of the time he lived indoors, in the hallway of our cramped apartment.

Because I was young and was accustomed to the dogs' natural freedom at the farm, I didn't understand the necessity of even walking Regalito. (I'd never seen anyone walk a dog in Mazatlán, after all.) Besides, the sidewalks were far too narrow, and the cars on our street came much too close to the houses. Since she feared for my safety, my mother wouldn't allow me to wander around out on the streets on my own. As a result, my little Regalito just got more and more aggravated and neurotic as the months passed.

Though we were making a new life for our family in the city, I think each of us was trying to re-create a simpler, more natural existence, like at the farm. I was trying the hardest, and I was failing. I needed to accept my circumstances, but instead, I fought them. I became like Regalito, barking his life away and jumping to see out the window. Or like one of the roof dogs, locked high above the streets, with only the laundry to amuse them.

Looking back, I'm struck by the similarity between my situation and that of Regalito and all those lonely roof dogs of Mazatlán. Just like them, I was physically and psychologically in a cage—repressed—and I felt like I could never just be me, my authentic self, anymore. As I watched those dogs act out their frustrations by pacing, jumping, and barking, I was acting out, too, but in different ways.

During those years, my dad was away at work almost all the time. We barely saw him. One day, my mother wanted me to be better behaved, so she told me, "You are the man of the house now." I bet she regretted it pretty quickly, because I really took it the wrong way. I began acting like a little Napoleon and trying to control everything. I used it as an excuse to pick on my sister Nora. I'd tease her, play pranks on her, and generally make her life miserable. My parents knew they had to rein me in somehow.

Today, when my clients have dogs that are acting out because of boredom or frustration—in other words, a lack of freedom—I often recommend that they take that pent-up energy and channel it in a positive, healthy way. Running the dogs next to you while you bike or rollerblade, taking the dogs swimming or on a long hike with a backpack in the mountains, introducing the active disciplines of lure coursing or agility training—all are ways to help give dogs a taste of that freedom that they crave but with structure and limits.

My parents did the same thing for me when they saw that I was beginning to act out my frustrations with the city in negative ways. They put me on my own program of agility training for humans. It was called karate. Starting at the age of seven, I took an after-school karate class that gave me a real physical outlet for my energy—as well as the kind of discipline and structure that I needed to be able to prioritize my responsibilities in life, such as going to school, doing my homework, caring for Regalito, and helping with the household chores. I often wonder what kind of person I'd be if my mom and dad hadn't caught on to the way I was feeling and acting. I probably wouldn't have grown up to become the disciplined, successful person I am today.

When it came to Regalito, I wish I'd understood then what I now know about how to give our domestic dogs a taste of freedom: the same things my parents understood about how to keep a high-energy, wound-up little boy in check.

I think we are drawn to dogs because they are the uninhibited creatures we might be if we weren't certain we knew better.
— George Bird Evans, author and dog breeder

Finding Your Personal Freedom

What does "freedom" mean to you? For my friend Jada Pinkett Smith, it can be as simple as the ability to spend hours in the hills alone hiking with her dogs, away from her cell phone, her business commitments, and the paparazzi. For my fiancée, Jahira, it's knowing I am safe and healthy when I travel far away from home. Freedom for her means freedom from worry. For my oldest son, Andre, it's relaxing on the beach and listening to music. For my youngest son, Calvin, it's having the time and space to create things: to draw pictures, design comic books, and write stories. Whenever I ask people what "freedom" means to them, I always get a different answer.

Dogs don't have to learn what freedom is; it's deep in their DNA. They act out their need for it all the time, and it's our job as their guardians to provide it as much as we possibly can. We humans act out our need for freedom, too; we just don't always know what we're seeking. Sometimes, it takes a little time to get it right.

Through my experiences working with people and their dogs, that stifled feeling many humans experience is not caused by physical boundaries, limitations of time, or laws governing our behavior. It's more likely to be caused by mental and emotional barriers that block our natural instincts and constrict our spirits. For instance, many of my clients will say, "My dog can never be around other dogs," or "My dog is totally untrainable." They don't realize they are placing arbitrary limits and constraints around another living being based on their own fears and self-doubts. It's up to me to show them that all these limitations begin in our minds. By placing such imaginary restrictions on their dogs, they are not only curbing their pet's freedom; they are also effectively eliminating their own.

When it comes to freedom, dogs know something most humans don't: Freedom comes from within. It's not a thing or a place; it's a state of being.

How Dogs Express Freedom

- By using their senses to explore and celebrate the world around them
- By accepting their place in the pack and understanding that consistent rules, boundaries, and limitations give them the freedom to be who they are

- ✅ By living in the moment, without regret about the past or anxiety about the future

- ✅ By expressing themselves as they are without shame and with no concern for how they look, sound, or smell

- ✅ By exercising their individual breed-specific skills, such as herding, chasing, retrieving, and tracking

The Encyclopedia of Dogs

By the time I was 9 or 10, I really felt like a fish out of water at school. The popular kids weren't that interested in me—and even if one of them did sit down with me at lunch, he'd get up and leave the moment someone more interesting came around.

With Regalito, I never had to worry about that. When I came rushing home to him after school, he'd greet me as if the most famous movie star in the world had just come in the room. He wasn't waiting for someone better to come around the corner—it was *me* and only me he wanted to be with. Regalito wanted to do whatever *I* wanted to do, whether it was playing hide-and-seek or running for miles along the beach. And if I simply wanted to sit quietly alone with my thoughts, Regalito was up for that, too. There was never any conflict, never any negotiating. We were truly best buddies, totally in tune with each other. Nobody understood him the way I did, and nobody understood me like Regalito.

I'd always been in love with animals, but my interest in dogs was now becoming a full-fledged passion. It seemed to me that there was this completely different species on

*Karate gave me a sense of self-confidence and security
as I adjusted to life in Mazatlán.*

Earth—made up of beings with paws, four legs, and tails—
with which I connected far better in spiritual and emotional
terms than I connected with any one human in my life. Dogs
had all the qualities—silent strength, adaptability, playful-
ness, determination, empathy, patience, and wisdom—that
I aspired to. I loved my family and knew they loved me—but
with dogs, I felt different. I felt whole.

When I turned 10, my mother gave me a copy of *The
Encyclopedia of Dogs* that she had ordered through the mail.
That book changed my life. When I opened its pages, a
wondrous new world suddenly was revealed to me. Most of
the dogs I'd seen in Mexico looked pretty similar—the same
gray-brown, scruffy, coyote-ish farm dogs. But inside my new
book, I saw hundreds of different dog breeds of all shapes
and sizes and colors—all exotic and rare gems to my eyes.

There was the Irish wolfhound, so enormous I could hardly believe it was real; the shar-pei, with its comically wrinkled face. And there was the St. Bernard, pictured in the midst of a hillside of snow—something I had never seen.

I wanted to know the history of how dogs evolved into the amazing animals they've become, how and when and where each breed was created and for what purpose. I wanted to meet and collect every dog of every breed that I read about in that book. I wanted them all to be my best friends, just like Regalito was.

Dogs are our link to paradise. They don't know evil or
jealousy or discontent. To sit with a dog on a hillside
on a glorious afternoon is to be back in Eden,
where doing nothing was not boring—it was peace.
—Milan Kundera

My First Purebred

I was walking home from school one day when I caught a glimpse of the first purebred dog I'd ever seen up close. She was a beautifully groomed Irish setter, with long, flowing reddish fur; flat, floppy ears; and a perfect, prancing runway gait. I knew she was an Irish setter, thanks to my *Encyclopedia,* which by this time was like my bible.

After snooping around a little, I learned that the Irish setter's owner was Dr. Carlos Guzman, who lived on the wealthy side of town. Dr. Guzman owned, raised, and showed prizewinning purebred Irish setters. He was the first person in Mazatlán I'd ever seen walking a dog, which he did every day at three o'clock. This man had become rich by performing illegal abortions, which were very much in demand in upper-class circles. My mother, a very devout Catholic, didn't approve of him for this reason—but all I cared about were his dogs. So I used to shadow him on his weekday walks. It became a ritual for me.

One day, I found the courage to approach Dr. Guzman. He would always walk the dog around the same time I would get out of school. In the past, I had waited until he had passed me on a street corner and then followed him at a distance. That afternoon, I actually chased him down the street; I must have scared him out of his wits! I went rushing after him down a steep and windy hill, and when I caught up, out of breath, I started asking him everything I could think of about his dog and the breed. It all came out in a rush.

After he got over his shock, Dr. Guzman smiled. I amused him—or, maybe, he saw my sincere passion for dogs, which was not a typical interest for a working-class Mexican boy. When I asked him if I could have one of his future puppies, his eyes twinkled and he agreed. (Of course, I knew that there would be puppies eventually, because at that time, no one in Mexico—and I mean no one—ever spayed or neutered their dogs. In Mexican culture, the thought of taking away any male's "manhood" is taboo—including if that male is a dog. It's a dangerous situation that I'm trying to improve by educating people that spaying and neutering is needed to reduce the number of abandoned and homeless dogs, which in America alone is estimated at more than six million.)

The puppy Dr. Guzman gave me was a female setter, and I named her Saluki. A Saluki is a sight hound, bred by ancient Egyptians; I was reading about them at the time. I liked the idea of naming my new dog, which looked a little like a Saluki, after one of the first recorded dog breeds in history. It made me feel connected to dogs in a way that honored their past.

Later, I figured out that Dr. Guzman gave me the "ugliest" dog in his litter. He liked to show his dogs, so he gave me the puppy that was the least likely to win any Irish setter beauty contests. Saluki was a big-boned girl and didn't have the graceful, feminized features of a show-quality Irish setter. Of course, I didn't know the difference—and even if I had, I wouldn't have cared. I was so excited and proud to have her for myself. To me, she was the most perfect, most beautiful dog in the world.

I surprised my mother when I came home with a new puppy, but she was always supportive of my passions. My dad was as obsessed with animals as I was, so he had no problem with it. And Regalito was happy to have a full-time friend to play with while I was at school.

Raising Saluki—the first purebred dog I had ever owned— gave me both joy and an even more heightened sense of responsibility. I was determined not to make the same mistakes I'd made with Regalito. I was beginning to catch on to what dogs needed to be happy in the city. More crucial than that, I was learning the importance of a sense of freedom— both for my dogs and for myself.

As Saluki got older, I started to walk her along with Regalito. I didn't like that Dr. Guzman walked his dogs on a leash. To my mind, that didn't give the animals enough freedom. Since there was no such thing as a leash law in Mexico back then, I could walk Saluki by my side, off-leash. Because I was fulfilling the most important aspect of her need for freedom and exercise—the drive to be outdoors, to smell things, to walk, and to migrate with her pack—it was easy to teach her to be perfectly obedient and to always follow right next to or behind me. The neighbors thought that it was some kind of magic trick. Like I said, dogs didn't follow people in Mexico.

For me, "Dog Days" symbolizes apocalyptic euphoria, chaotic freedom, and running really, really fast with your eyes closed.
—Florence Welch, of Florence and the Machine,
on her hit song "Dog Days Are Over"

A House by the Beach

My father worked long, hard hours as a freelance photographer and cameraman. When I turned 12, he had managed to save up enough money to purchase a little house for us in Mazatlán, just two blocks from the beach. It had a front yard for the dogs and more room for our growing family, which now included me, Nora, my youngest sister, Monica, and my brand-new baby brother, Erick.

Moving to the new house helped me feel like my kennel doors were finally opening. Being able to hear the roar of the ocean nearby felt primal and natural, and I relished its sound and its smells. It smelled like freedom, and the future.

Of course, I took both dogs with me. Regalito was getting on in age, but he had become a much happier dog since I'd started learning more about how to fulfill his needs, and since I'd been walking him with Saluki. Both of them were instantly even happier away from our cramped, second-floor apartment.

I learned a lot about hard work and compassion from my parents,
who have always been my biggest supporters and fans.

As I got older and began going farther and farther from my neighborhood to explore the city on my own, I would run into people who would ask me about my dogs, which went everywhere with me. Pretty soon, I'd become known as that kid who was dog crazy. It worked in my favor though, because when someone would have an extra puppy, they'd ask me if I wanted it. I'd never say no. I'd also peruse the classified ads for people who were selling dogs or puppies. My parents, delighted that I'd found my passion, were happy to oblige my new interest.

There was Kitsey, an Alaskan mix; Oso, a Samoyed; and Ozzie, a husky. I started walking them together more and more—off-leash, as a pack—and gradually, I witnessed their personalities blossom as they became more relaxed, more social, and more like the dogs I knew at the farm. In many ways, this was my first hands-on lesson in dog behavior. I saw that when I offered my dogs even the smallest taste of the freedom that is their birthright, they would return my gift many times over with their obedience, loyalty, and affection. For me back then, freedom began to feel like walking through the streets of Mazatlán or running on the beach, followed by my pack of beautiful, perfectly behaved dogs.

Once again, my family accepted every new family member with joy. My mother used to say, "I'll just put more water in the beans," and when my father was home, he'd always go around to all the local taco places at closing time to ask for their leftovers.

Love and Freedom

My little Regalito lived to be all of 12 years old and died a quiet, natural death in that house by the beach—not bad for a dog that spent the majority of his life trapped in a hot, dusty little apartment and ate mostly leftovers (dog food was a First World item).

Sometimes, remembering Regalito makes me sad. I discovered early on that many of a dog's behavior problems stem from being cooped up all day, and I swore I'd never let that happen to any of my dogs again. I know I did the best I could for him, but still, if I could, I'd apologize to my very first dog. Even though I was only a small boy who didn't know any better, I wish I could turn back the clock and set Regalito free to run for miles on the beach, or send him back to my grandfather's farm, where he could have lived out his life naturally, with the rest of my grandfather's pack.

Of course, the only way to make it up to Regalito now is to help as many other dogs as I can, so they never have to live constrained lives, even in our unnatural human world. I want to help all dogs experience their own definitions of "freedom" and live a life that fully expresses the natural animal that they are.

True love means supporting and helping another person or animal accomplish something that is important to them: to fulfill their desires before thinking of your own. Dogs show us love all the time by being hypersensitive to our needs and trying their best to satisfy our human needs for companionship, love, and obedience. But while we always say we "love our dogs," too often we treat them as if they exist only for our pleasure and convenience. We ignore their very real inborn needs and desires — for exercise, discipline, and affection. Too often, my clients give affection, affection, and affection, because it's easier and it's what they want in the moment. I try to teach them that to truly love a dog, you must learn to fulfill that animal's necessities before your own.

What if we take the formula for success with dogs that I have used with hundreds of clients and apply it to our relationships with people? What if we put aside our selfish desires and attempt to understand what other people — spouse, friend, partner, child, parent, employee, boss — need to make them happy first? What if we stop trying to control people and situations and instead watch and listen to what they are really trying to tell us? Wouldn't that go a long way in helping everyone that we touch experience a little more peace and freedom in their lives?

Sting famously sang, "If you love someone, set them free." As any parent will tell you, that's not an easy thing to do. In my life right now, the greatest challenge facing me every day is to let my sons, Andre and Calvin, be free to make their own mistakes without my intervention. I tell myself that I am fulfilling their needs by trying to help them in their careers, putting them through school, and giving them advice. In reality, much of that is for me—it's selfishly what I need to feel like a good father. But what do my boys themselves need? As tough as it might be for me to accept, sometimes, they need me to let go and allow them to sink or swim on their own.

For example, my eldest son, Andre, lived with my ex-wife during the ugliest period of our divorce. Becoming the de facto "man of the house," he decided he was mature enough to move out on his own—despite the fact that he hadn't yet graduated from high school. He believed he could have his own apartment, take full care of himself, and still pass all his high school classes and graduation exams.

I strongly disagreed with his choice, but he wasn't hearing it, and I had to learn to bite my tongue to preserve my then-fragile relationship with him. That year—as I'd predicted—Andre failed his final exams and wasn't able to graduate with his class. When the reality hit him, he finally buckled down on his studies and was ultimately granted a GED certificate. But it wasn't the same thing as the once-in-a-lifetime experience of wearing the cap and gown, marching to the dais with his class, and celebrating this important life milestone with his friends and peers. Andre regrets it now; but if I hadn't let him have the freedom to make his own mistake, we probably wouldn't even be speaking today.

Then there's Calvin, my youngest son, who is the most like me: the most curious, the most disruptive, the most rebellious, the most anti-authority.

When he was 16, Calvin landed his Nickelodeon TV show, *Mutt and Stuff,* a scripted children's show about a school for (puppet) dogs. At this stage, he had only taken a total of three months' worth of acting lessons in his life. When it came time to tape the first episodes, he was given scripts and was told to practice and memorize his lines in advance of filming.

Well, Calvin felt those three short months of acting lessons meant he could skip the rest of the hard work and just show up on set and be brilliant. Even though I offered many times to run his lines with him, Calvin told me that he had everything under control and that once he arrived on set, everything would immediately fall into place. It took everything I had to bite my tongue, let him make his own mistakes, and not warn him that he was likely putting his entire series at risk.

Sure enough, when the first day of filming arrived, Calvin was woefully unprepared. Again and again, he kept messing up or completely forgetting his lines. This went on for the first several weeks of filming. The show director became increasingly frustrated with him, to the point where he told the producers that they should fire Calvin and replace him with a *professional* child actor.

That was the wake-up call Calvin needed. Once his job was on the line, he buckled down, learned his lines, and focused on preparing to deliver the best show possible. The result: In its first year on the air, the show was nominated for two Daytime Emmy awards, including best preschool show. Even though I'd warned him about what might happen if he didn't practice, I think it's in all teenagers' DNA not to believe their parents. I'm glad I held in my anger and frustration until Calvin had learned that very hard lesson on his own.

As for me? My definition of "freedom" has evolved throughout my life. I think of freedom the way a dog does. When my level of respect is high, my trust increases. When my trust increases, my loyalty is stronger.

Dogs have also taught me that a sense of freedom is essential for a balanced life. Watch how your dog's true, best nature comes out when you click off her leash and let her run free through a field. Now close your eyes and imagine that for yourself—living life "off-leash" from your self-imposed limitations and fears.

Dog Lesson #2
How to Experience Freedom

- Follow your passion and obey your instincts. Your passion creates the energy that fuels your accomplishments, and your instincts are the compass that guides you through life's challenges.

- Notice when you feel sad, confused, frustrated, or anxious. These emotions create limitations, and experiencing them persistently could be a signal to make a change in your life. Repressed emotions can actually cause physical illnesses if you don't pay attention to them.

- Be honest with yourself about who you really are. When our self-image is an illusion, then we are destined to disappoint ourselves and others.

- Accept when it's time to surrender to situations that you can't control.

LESSON 3:
CONFIDENCE

It is best to act with confidence, no matter
how little right you have to it.
—Lillian Hellman

Daisy was a jet-black cocker spaniel with shining black eyes that looked into mine with suspicion one late-winter afternoon in 1991. The day that we first met, her fur was overgrown, dirty, and a little matted. Long strands of it fell over her eyes and I noticed her nails were curling deep into her paws.

Though Daisy was trembling when I took her in my arms, I remember my brand-new bosses—Miss Nancy and Miss Martha, the joint owners of Chula Vista Grooming—looking at each other nervously. They were no doubt hoping that the dog wouldn't attack me the way she'd attacked them in the past. I heard them talking to each other in nervous voices, but I couldn't understand a word they were saying. The only English I knew at that point was "Do you have application for work?"

It didn't matter, because I understood someone in that room perfectly—even better, in fact, than if she'd been speaking Spanish to me. It was Daisy herself. No one else could see it, but she was already telling me everything I needed to know about her.

All the distractions faded, and suddenly it was just the two of us. I realized that I felt calmer and more confident than I had since I'd crossed the border into the United States just a few weeks earlier. I looked at Daisy and ran my hands over her fur. She looked back at me, and her trembling stopped.

I moved her to the grooming table and got ready to begin.

Dogs do speak, but only to those who know how to listen.
—Orhan Pamuk

Crossing the River

I've written before about coming to America, about crossing the Rio Grande to a new life. I arrived with enough money in my pocket to make it to what I thought was San Diego (in reality, it was Chula Vista, about 10 miles away). Reporters and interviewers have transformed this experience into the quintessential "immigrant with nothing makes good" tale. But that's not the whole story. Nobody ever writes about the fear and insecurity that went along with it.

During my teenage years, my growing interest in dogs was helping me form a picture of what my future might look like. I used to watch the American shows on television—*Lassie, Rin Tin Tin,* and *The Little Rascals*—and was amazed by what these canine "actors" could do. Because of my deep connection with dogs, I knew in my heart that I wanted to build a career working with animals, teaching them to do amazing things for the camera. Of course, this would not be possible in Mexico, given the cultural lack of respect for dogs. I had no idea how I would achieve this, but I became determined to go to America and become a dog trainer for Hollywood.

It was a couple of weeks after Christmas. I was 21, cold, wet, hungry, and far away from my parents and siblings in Mazatlán and my grandparents in Culiacán. Just south of the U.S. border, I stood in the Rio Grande with icy, muddy water up to my chest. Beside me stood the coyote I had paid to transport me to my new life. ("Coyote" is the name Mexicans give to someone who helps people cross the border illegally.) I desperately wanted to make it to the other side—where I could attain my American dream of becoming the best dog trainer in the world.

By the time it was past midnight and completely dark, I was beginning to have second thoughts. "Coyote" was in fact a good description for my guide, because he had the same skinny, hungry look as the animal. He had already taken all my money—the hundred dollars my father had given me on Christmas Eve—and for all I knew, he was planning to kill me. Still, I felt I had no choice. I followed his whispered instructions until, finally: "*¡Corre!*—Run!"

He led me into a dark, low, narrow tunnel, and I thought, "This is where he's going to kill me." In that moment, there were only three things I could trust: the coyote, God, and myself. It was a pure leap of faith.

Obviously, the coyote didn't kill me; he got me across the border safely. But I didn't feel the elation I had expected once I set foot on American soil. Instead, the realities of my situation came flooding in. I had no money. I didn't speak the language. I had no food and nowhere to live. And I had no idea where to begin.

My teen years in Mazatlán were challenging for me. I was not the most secure kid, but there were two things in the world that I felt really confident about: my karate skills and my ability with dogs. But spending most of your time around dogs was not something that was considered "normal" by our Mexican culture—and especially by my classmates. The kids would ridicule me, calling me *"el perrero*—dirty dog boy,"* bullying me, and whispering about me behind my back while excluding me from their social circles. I was able to survive their constant

 FROM THE SCIENCE FILES

The Science of Confidence

According to the *Journal of Personality and Social Psychology,* simply owning a dog can build confidence in humans. In a paper titled "Friends With Benefits: On the Positive Consequences of Pet Ownership," lead researcher Allen R. McConnell describes long-term studies that found pet owners had greater self-esteem, were more physically fit, tended to be less lonely, were more conscientious and extroverted, and were less fearful and preoccupied than those without pets.[2] A second experiment using only dog owners found an even greater sense of well-being, as dogs increased their owners' feelings of belonging, self-esteem, and having a meaningful existence.

taunts because I had my dogs waiting for me at home, always ready to give me unconditional love and companionship.

Despite the fact that I always felt different from my class-mates, I still had a strong inner passion that propelled me forward. A voice deep inside me told me I had a special gift and never to give up. Since I graduated high school in Mazatlán, I'd become good at trusting my instincts to find the right path to get me where I wanted to be—like securing a job as a groomer and technician with one of the few veterinarians in town.

Now, grimy and starving in this strange, intimidating new country called America, I feared my confidence was desert-ing me.

Bottom of the Pack

When I arrived in California, I knew that making it in Amer-ica was not going to be easy, but I was still excited by the adventure of it all. There were so many new things to see, to learn, and to explore.

Right off the bat, I had to find a way to make enough money to feed myself. I'd wander the streets of Chula Vista, stopping at different stores and asking, "Do you have appli-cation for work?" Various businesspeople would give me a couple of dollars for sweeping their sidewalks, storerooms, or garages. It wasn't exactly a confidence builder, but the hard work made me feel a little better about myself.

I quickly learned that, in America, the best way to get work is to take on the jobs Americans would rather not do. That meant washing cars, washing windows, sweeping floors, and hosing down parking lots and sidewalks. For the first three months, I slept at a homeless camp I found hidden beneath a freeway. I also discovered the joy of 25-cent hot dogs from 7-Eleven.

After a few weeks in Chula Vista, the optimism I'd brought with me across the border began to fade. I tried to fight the feeling, but I can admit it now: I was afraid. I still had no clue how I would make a real life for myself in this foreign place. I wandered the streets, trying to come up with a plan. Some people scowled at me as if I were dirty and didn't belong. I had never felt more like I was at the very bottom of the pack. I kept wondering, "What am I doing here? What do I even have to offer this place called America?"

In Mexico, we are conditioned to think that Americans know everything and are the best in the world. After all, we are constantly seeing movies in which America saves the world.

I started working in America at a grooming salon,
but soon I was training my first canine clients.

FROM THE CELEBRITY FILES

Wayne Brady

Actor, singer, comedian, and host of TV's *Let's Make a Deal,* Wayne Brady confides that the extroverted showman he seems to be on TV is a far cry from the more reserved person he is off-screen. "I would never describe myself as a socially gregarious person," he says. "I come across a certain way on stage 'cause that's my job ... but I don't think you should ever confuse someone's job with their true personality."

Wayne says that he's been an introvert since he was a boy, wary of social occasions and meeting new people: "It's very easy for you, if you're not a social person, to sit back and isolate. Not to get too deep with it, but it really does stem from, as a child, being in situations where I felt bullied. Eventually I learned to stand up for myself and have a voice—but it was already ingrained in me not to mix. Because if you speak to somebody, if you say something to them, there's an opportunity for that person to say something harmful back or to treat you in a manner that would make you uncomfortable."

Wayne's Rottweiler, Charlie, changed all that for him. "I look at my dog, Charlie, who can walk into a room and go up to the one person who's probably the least-happy, least-smiling guy and just give him her paw to shake," he says. "The fact that she's so open and so willing to be loved and so willing to put herself out ... that's taught me something. It doesn't cost me anything to walk up to somebody and say hi and introduce myself and smile. That's the lesson that I learned from Charlie. And I try to practice that as much as I can, because it doesn't come to me naturally. She has inspired me to open myself up that way."

(I don't remember any movies in which Mexico saves the world, do you?) On the other hand, some Americans are brought up to think that Mexican immigrants are second-class citizens. At that time of my life, I felt like I was even less than that.

Help Wanted

My perspective began to change when I saw the "Help Wanted" sign in the window of a small white storefront that said "Grooming." (I understood what kind of business it was since there were pictures of a dog, a hairbrush, and a blow-dryer on the door.) I had worked as a groomer in a vet's office for two years in Mazatlán, so here was a real skill that I actually could put to use.

The problem was how to convince the owners to hire me. I didn't have any papers, a home address, or a social security number, and I didn't even speak English. I went inside to the reception area and saw two older women, probably around 60, behind the counter. They were very down-to-earth: gray hair, no makeup, and wearing plain, loose, unpretentious clothes. They introduced themselves as Martha and Nancy. I later learned that they had owned and run Chula Vista Grooming for more than 20 years, and it was a fixture in the neighborhood.

I used my only English—"Do you have application for work?"—and filled out the form they handed me as best I could. They looked at my half-filled application, and then at me. But instead of handing me a broom or a mop, like my previous employers had, Miss Nancy handed me a photograph of what a perfectly groomed cocker spaniel should look like. I examined it and nodded. Miss Nancy then looked at Miss Martha, who motioned me into a back room.

In the room were grooming tools, an industrial blow-dryer, a tub, a metal table ... and a little black cocker spaniel cowering and growling in a low, threatening tone. It was Daisy.

Regaining My Confidence

I'll never know why these two women decided to trust a scrawny 21-year-old Mexican immigrant who'd just come in off the streets. I also didn't know anything about their history with the dog. It was only much later that I learned that Daisy had been terrorizing both the groomers and her owners for months, and they considered her a lost cause.

I only know what happened next.

Miss Nancy and Miss Martha watched in amazement as Daisy stopped trembling the minute I took her in my hands. Although they were regarding her with fear, as if she were a monster, I could see right away she wasn't a naturally aggressive dog. She was just insecure.

For me, energy and an animal's body language deliver a dog's dialogue as clearly as language does any human's—and I was immediately engaged in an intense conversation with Daisy. She was speaking directly to me, showing me with her posture and movements that there were places on her body where she felt uncomfortable being touched by strangers. Naturally, I avoided those places—her rear end, her stomach—and instead, I lifted gently under her chin and shifted her upright, to a very proud position. I knew instinctively that I had to build up her trust and confidence in order to groom her. She responded instantly, as if to say, "Thank you—finally someone is listening to me!" Then I began to clip.

Watching Daisy's insecurities melt away made all those weeks of my own self-doubt vanish right along with them. For the first time since I'd left Mexico, I felt my confidence returning. I truly did have something to offer—and by the way my potential employers were looking at me, it was clearly something these Americans really needed!

I finished grooming Daisy and handed her back. Miss Nancy and Miss Martha looked astonished, but happy. So happy! They went to the cash register and took out $60 and handed it to me. I shook my head and pushed it back toward them, trying to communicate "too much." They nodded encouragingly and pointed to the price chart on the wall, showing me that I was getting half the $120 price for Daisy's makeover. All my previous jobs in America had been onetime only, but the store owners pointed to the calendar, indicating for me to return the next day.

By the following week, word had spread to regular clients of Chula Vista Grooming that there was a boy named Cesar in the house who could work with even the most difficult dogs. Clients saw their dogs leaving the grooming sessions happy instead of stressed-out. Suddenly, people weren't scowling at me anymore. They were smiling and thanking me when I'd come out of the back room with their well-cared-for, peaceful dogs. All those grateful smiles built up my self-confidence, too.

Over the following months, my new bosses and I communicated in broken Spanish, along with a lot of pointing and the few new English words I was learning: "wash," "dryer," "clippers." My bosses gave me their key and let me sleep and wash myself inside the office. That, and earning half the profits from all my grooming jobs, allowed me to save money and to make a logical plan for becoming a professional dog trainer.

Ultimately, I decided I would need to move north to Los Angeles, where all the Hollywood dog trainers lived and worked. Sadly, that meant leaving the safe haven of Chula Vista Grooming after nine months.

I was and always will be indebted to Miss Nancy and Miss Martha, who took a chance on me. Since I still didn't know much English, the only way I could tell them I was leaving for good was by handing them back their keys. I'm glad I had learned the words "thank you."

HOW DOGS DEVELOP CONFIDENCE

- By knowing their position in their group or family. Being accepted into a pack makes them feel secure.

- By mastering a skill. It can be something as simple as retrieving, swimming, or fetching—or something more complex, like herding or agility.

- By having a role model to follow, play, and explore with

- By developing a sense of security—in their environment, their pack, and their life. Fearful dogs can't have confidence until they have a sense of security.

By facing and overcoming challenges and constantly learning new skills. (This is why police and military dogs are so confident: They face a lot of challenges other dogs never do.)

Out of the Comfort Zone

When I am rehabilitating an insecure dog, I try to gradually ease the animal out of its comfort zone, continually introducing new challenges and using my own confidence or the confidence of another dog in my pack to shore up the insecure dog.

Most parents know that, in the human world, every new achievement—even the smallest one—builds new strength and self-reliance in a child. It works the same way for dogs.

To help our pets work through their anxieties, we must strive to be strong, consistent role models they can trust, because trust builds confidence, too. The miracle is that when you build a dog's confidence, you build your own even more. If you're not confident about your relationship with your dog, you can't be a real role model. When you learn to assertively lead, guide, and care for a dog, it's that old law of the universe at work: What you give, you get back a thousandfold.

Canine Confidence Artists

The beauty of dogs is that the gift of confidence is reciprocal. This means that the more you become a strong leader to your dog, the more your own confidence will grow. I have dozens of clients who are as famous and successful as the Seinfelds (see Celebrity File, opposite), but who instantly

FROM THE CELEBRITY FILES

Jerry Seinfeld

"I'm beloved by millions," moaned Jerry Seinfeld, a client and friend who never fails to make me laugh. "Except for one little dog."

Jerry confessed that he was having issues with one of his two dachshunds, José and Foxy. Foxy was unfriendly with Jerry and seemed afraid of him (and any other adult male, for that matter). "Jerry has basically written her off," his wife, Jessica, told me one afternoon.

The Seinfelds were first-time dog owners and didn't feel at all confident about how to behave around their new pets. This insecurity weakened them in their dogs' eyes; dogs are less likely to obey or respect a self-doubting human. My solution was to not only build self-esteem in the shy Foxy but also to bolster the confidence of her famous owners as well.

First, to build the dog's confidence, I used a leash, allowing her to come toward me, baby step by baby step. By the end of the exercise, she was tentatively but curiously investigating my leg.

Now for the owners: I assigned Jerry to be the one to reward her for her bravery. This meant that Jerry had to move past his own fears and be close to her, giving praise and affection.

I also showed the Seinfelds a different way of walking Foxy to increase her self-esteem: by letting her lead the parade of the family "pack." The more challenges the Seinfelds give Foxy in the future, the more she will overcome her fears and build self-confidence.

By challenging Foxy and sharing in her progress and accomplishments, Jerry increased his own confidence as a dog owner by leaps and bounds.

FROM THE SCIENCE FILES

Reading to Dogs Builds Confidence and Literacy in Kids

The fact that dogs accept us as we are and don't judge us the way other humans often do is part of why being around them helps us feel calmer, more secure, and more confident. Researchers have been studying the effect that simply reading aloud to a quiet, attentive dog has on children with low literacy skills or other learning disabilities. Their early findings are promising.[3] The evidence suggests that children who read to dogs have improved reading performance overall, although more research is needed to explain exactly how and why this phenomenon occurs.

relinquish all their power with their dogs the moment they come home.

That isn't the way it's supposed to be. When we base our self-esteem on our success and material possessions, then confidence can be fleeting and paper-thin. Financial success can come and go. But being a calm, assertive leader to your dog is an ability that flows from the inside out. That's the kind of confidence that never goes away.

When it comes to our insecurities, we all have sensitive spots. Daisy's were on her body—the places she didn't want a groomer to touch. My sensitive spot was my insecurity, rooted in my belief that I was not good enough in a strange new country.

We all have areas of strength, too. Daisy's was under her chin. My strength was a deeper understanding of dog communication that my bosses—even as dog lovers—didn't share. Daisy and the other dogs I groomed showed me that, yes, I did have something special to offer: something that my adopted new country really needed.

As I learned from Daisy, the best way to build confidence is to earn trust and respect from others. This is the spark that begins to create self-assurance. I believe dogs can help us find the instinctual strength that resides within each one of us.

 Dog Lesson #3
How to Build Self-Confidence

- ✅ Use dogs as your role models. Dogs just want to be dogs—not another animal, and certainly not human. Use their example to honor and take pride in who you are.

- ✅ Seek your own special inborn gift or talent, nurture it, and work on it until you master it. Competence builds confidence.

- ✅ View the toughest challenges in your life as opportunities to build inner strength. The more difficulties you overcome, the more confident you will be.

- ✅ Never stop learning. Take every opportunity you can to tackle a new skill and discover new abilities.

LESSON 4:
AUTHENTICITY

Questers of the truth, that's who dogs are;
seekers after the invisible scent of
another being's authentic core.
—Jeffrey Moussaieff Masson, *Dogs Never Lie About Love*

P erhaps the most profound lesson I have learned from dogs is that of *authenticity*. When we can live our lives from a place where we don't hide our inner feelings, when we don't create illusions about who we really are, when we approach every challenge in life with candor, and when we can bravely admit our mistakes and learn from them, the human experience will be richer and more rewarding than we could ever imagine.

Dogs live in that world every day. They have always lived there. Because dogs simply cannot lie.

What is authenticity? To me, it's almost the same thing as honesty, but about a hundred times more powerful. To animals, authenticity is normal. Many animals are capable of deception as a survival strategy—for instance, a mother bird may fake a broken wing to divert a predator away from her nest. But only we humans are actually able to lie to *ourselves.*

We humans wear masks every day: masks to cover up our secret shames, masks to raise our self-esteem with others, masks that help us deny that we're doing something that isn't good for us or that might be hurtful to another person. Those masks are often two-sided—one side to fool the world; the other, to fool ourselves. *Humans are the only animals capable of denial, the practiced art of lying to one's self.*

When you are being authentic, you face *all* the different truths about yourself, even the ones you'd rather not see or expose. When you are authentic, you are being true to others—and, more important, true to the essence of who you really are.

In the realm of animal instincts, authenticity has a feel to it. It has an energy and a smell; all dogs know instantly when someone or something is being authentic or not. But in the intellectual realm where most humans dwell, authenticity is much harder to determine.

Authenticity and Energy

One of the first rules of authenticity is that its measure is inseparable from the *energy* any animal or person projects. Let me take a moment to explain my concept of energy as it relates to our communication with dogs, other animals, and each other.

"Energy," as I define it, is composed of two elements: emotion and intention. The truer we are to our intentions and feelings, the stronger an energy we project. Our dogs soak it all up like sponges—precisely because it's been their evolutionary duty to make sense of our ever-changing human condition.

Dogs know immediately if our intentions don't match our emotional state. This was evident during one of my recent cases. A client came to me when his three Rottweilers became out of control during their evening walks, so I decided to observe him. As it turned out, the owner was on his mobile phone during most of the walk and was clearly agitated by some of his conversations. He wasn't being present with his dogs, and was certainly not paying attention when the dogs were pulling and lunging at passersby.

When I questioned him afterward, my client admitted that he deliberately saved his most contentious phone conversations for those evening walks. He wanted to be out of the house so his family would not hear him yell or become agitated. Thus, his real intention was not to go for a casual evening walk with his dogs, but to escape the house so he could deal with stressful business situations. Because his intentions were not honest, his energy on the walk was weak, and his Rottweilers became the terrors of the neighborhood.

This is what I mean when I say the energy you create is formed by your emotions and your intentions. My client's emotions and intentions were out of alignment. His emotion was anger and upset. His intention was to escape his home so that he could have privacy. He was not clearly being authentic. And the outcome was an out-of-control pack.

I had many canine teachers of authenticity over the years, but two very different Rottweilers stand out: one called Cycle and another called Cain. They both came into my life during the years when I was feeling my way and discovering what shape my professional path would take.

If a dog ... will not come to you after he has looked you in the face,
you ought to go home and examine your conscience.
—Woodrow Wilson

Cleaning Kennels

After I said goodbye to my guardian angels at Chula Vista Grooming, I made my way to Los Angeles, where I pounded the pavement, searching for employment at every dog-training company in the city. Finally, I got an interview to be a kennel boy at All-American Dog Training Academy. It was the type of facility where people would pay a lot of money for dogs to be impeccably trained and 100 percent obedient in just two weeks. In my broken English, I was able to express to the owner that I aspired to be a dog trainer. He hired me on the spot—not to train dogs, but to clean the kennels.

Day in and day out, I scraped and scrubbed and hosed down those kennels until they sparkled. Growing up on a farm had given me a powerful work ethic. My grandfather taught me that if you take on a job, you do it reliably, to the best of your ability, and see it through. I carried that philosophy with me from Mexico to America, and it was this dedication and work ethic that had endeared me to Miss Martha and Miss Nancy at Chula Vista Grooming.

At All-American, I worked even harder. Of course, I hoped my diligence would be noticed and that one day, I'd be promoted to assistant trainer. At the same time, I was learning as much as I could by observing the professional trainers who worked there.

So much of what I saw just didn't sit right with me. While the dogs that arrived at the facility were obviously loved, well cared for, and in top condition, their behavior told another story. I saw fear, frustration, an inability to focus, and even out-of-control aggression. The owners had paid a lot of money to bring their dogs to this place in the hopes of "curing" them of these problem behaviors. But I quickly saw that learning how to sit, stay, come, and heel did nothing to address these deeper behavioral issues. The dogs were kept in isolated kennels between lessons, and that only added to their sense of anxiety and instability.

In my weeks at All-American, I got to know a few of the trainers who worked alongside me. They were all good people who really cared about animals—but the problem was one of time and money. When you have promised a client that you will give them a perfectly obedient dog in two weeks, you have to do what it takes to make that happen. That often meant taking shortcuts, even when the animals were stressed-out: crouched down, ears back. Any parent knows that being conditioned to respond to a command under those circumstances won't do a thing to improve a child's overall behavior—let alone rehabilitate a dog.

That observation alone was a mini-lesson in authenticity. I began to understand that traditional *training*—sit, stay, come, heel—is created for the human, using human language and a human way of learning. Dogs, on the other hand, have no ambition to become human; they just want to be dogs, and to relate to their humans as their authentic selves.

From Dirty Kennels to Dirty Cars

Little by little, my boss at All-American gave me more responsibilities. One of my jobs was to bring the dogs from their kennels to their lessons. The trainers soon noticed that I was able to handle even the impossible behavioral problems. I had no fear of the most powerful breeds, and they sensed this and naturally followed me. With the extremely fearful dogs, I never yelled or used any force. I would simply sit with them in their kennels for as long as it took until they relaxed, then got curious about me. Trust established, they'd approach me and let me put the leash on them.

The fact that I could handle these extreme cases meant that even though they didn't consider me one of them, the trainers would sometimes turn their most stubborn dogs over to me.

One of All-American's clients, a man named Ross, was particularly impressed with my progress in training his dog, a burly Rottweiler named Cycle (after Ross's love of motor-

The first dogs I trained were two Rottweilers whose owners wanted to keep them as personal protection dogs.

cycles). Observing that I was underappreciated, Ross offered me a job washing cars at a limousine service he owned. He said he would pay me much better than my salary at All-American and would even give me a "company car"—something I desperately needed to get around the vast city of Los Angeles. On the side, he wanted me to continue to train Cycle, whom he was planning to use as a personal protection dog.

More than a decade later, I would learn that Ross had a good reason for wanting protection: Behind his slick facade and the front of his legitimate business, he was selling drugs. He was later arrested and served time in jail for his crimes.

On the face of it, leaving this highly respected dog-training academy to wash cars would seem like a giant step in the wrong direction. But I went with my gut, which proved to be right. As long as I got all my car-washing work done, Ross said I could train other dogs in addition to Cycle. Before I even had time to wonder where my new clients would come from, I learned that a lot of well-connected Hollywood people came to Ross to rent limousines for special occasions. Whenever any celebrities or their employees would show up for a car, Ross would go on and on about this Mexican guy who worked for him and was amazing with dogs.

It wasn't long before some of those big name limo renters were showing up at Ross's place—Vin Diesel, Nicolas Cage, and Michael Bay—to find me up to my armpits in suds. When they offered me work training their dogs, I always said yes. I took on as many dogs as I could realistically manage at once. I usually had about 10; the most I ever took on was 13 (which was a little bit insane). But I not only needed the money; I also wanted the challenge. I was in the early stages of developing my methods, learning what worked and

FROM THE SCIENCE FILES

Everybody Lies

Social and forensic research by Dr. Leanne ten Brinke, a forensic psychologist at the Haas School of Business at the University of California, Berkeley, suggests that humans are particularly incompetent at determining whether a person is lying or telling the truth. In fact, it appears that our judgments are no more accurate than the flip of a coin.[4]

This is concerning, since deception and inauthenticity seem to have taken over our culture. There's a saying among cynical law enforcement and judiciary professionals that "everybody lies," and a study by J. T. Hancock, an expert in deception and technology at Stanford University, seems to indicate that it's true.[5] It's estimated that we humans lie in 14 percent of our emails, 37 percent of phone conversations, and 27 percent of face-to-face conversations—and that's just with people we care about the most!

what didn't. And the only way to do that was to practice, practice, practice.

Authenticity: Let Cycle Be Cycle!

Cycle was the first dog to teach me why authenticity is essential, in both the dog world and the human one.

Ross had charged me with turning Cycle into a ferocious guardian. I had always enjoyed the high-energy challenge and physicality of personal-protection training, but the more I got to know this dog, the less I wanted to do that kind of work with him. Cycle was a very intelligent guy, quick to pick up on the concepts and commands. And he clearly was eager to give me what I asked from him. But after only about a week working with Cycle, I could see that while he was the right breed for the role of a guard dog, he simply didn't have the right energy.

Just as any dog can be rehabilitated and brought back to balance, any dog can be trained. Most dog owners know how smart and versatile the species is, and how attuned they are to human wants and needs. But that doesn't mean that the training objectives in question are necessarily the right fit. Just as forcing a child who was born to paint to focus only on mathematics, or forcing a quiet child who'd rather be reading to try out for sports, forcing a dog into a mold that only the human wants generally doesn't have a very positive outcome.

Dogs are individuals, but very often, their DNA and breeding determine what activities will be right for them. Take greyhounds, for instance. A greyhound is a sight hound, known for its ability to run distances and chase lures. Teaching it to track or hunt may be a more complicated proposition than teaching a beagle, which is a scent hound and naturally gravitates to this activity. Chances are, the greyhound wouldn't even be very interested in tracking. The opposite would be true of the beagle, which can be taught to chase a lure but will probably do it only halfheartedly, because she'd far rather be keeping her nose to the ground and picking up scents.

However, as in Cycle's case, the energy is every bit as important as the breed when it comes to understanding what a dog is best suited to do. I have a saying: "The energy is the energy." What I mean by this is that the energy that a dog is born with can't be changed by human will or training. (Humans might call this energy "personality," but a dog sees it as his natural place in his environment and in his pack.)

According to this philosophy, a low-energy dog will be lackluster at certain tasks suited for a high-energy dog—for example, scaring off a determined burglar—no matter how well he's been trained. And by the same token, a high-energy, dominant dog may be able to learn the basic skills to become a gentle, tolerant therapy dog—but he is not going to be a very helpful or happy one.

Like most Rotties, Cycle had the muscular build and imposing square jaw that looks intimidating. But on the inside, he was just a sweet, bumbling, playful guy—a solid middle-of-the-pack dog. He had energy to burn, but he didn't take well to confrontation. It just wasn't in him.

For a dog to excel at personal protection, he has to be born a confident pack leader. This is the kind of dog that becomes a K9 police officer. Those dogs have the instinct to put themselves in front of harm's way. If they're shot at, they have to keep coming at the bad guy. They can't be the type to startle at loud noises or run away when someone surprises them from behind a door. They just keep moving forward until their handler tells them to stop.

Cycle wasn't like that. He didn't mind protection training, because he loved learning new things—but he viewed it as only a game. He was a lighthearted spirit who just wanted to play.

Because Cycle couldn't be his authentic self under this training regimen, the work began to feel more like programming a robot than bringing out his best qualities. I had a problem on my hands. I wanted to please Ross and do what he had hired me to do, but I wasn't working with a piece of machinery. I was working with an individual: a living, feeling dog.

One day, while I was washing a limo and struggling over what to do about Cycle's training, I accidentally stumbled on his real talent: He was incredibly clever at learning complex tasks and tricks. What's more, he really loved that kind of interaction with me.

Unlike the protection training, which he did only because I wanted him to, I could tell that Cycle was self-motivated and eager to learn other behaviors that would be more in tune with his happy-go-lucky personality. Since I wanted to maximize my time with the dogs I was working with, I started to invent little games for some of them to do while I was busy washing cars. One day, I hit upon the idea of teaching an intelligent German shepherd named Howie to be my "assistant." Over a period of a few weeks, I taught him to bring me a bucket of water when I asked for it. It occurred to me that now that I had a bucket boy, maybe I should try to teach Cycle how to carry the hose.

Cycle proved to be an amazingly adept student. It was like he had been waiting all his life to learn this stuff! He was so big and had such a powerful jaw that my biggest problem was teaching him not to puncture the hose with his teeth when he pulled it. Ross made me replace every hose he punctured, and on my small salary, that was a big hit. Eventually, I had Cycle not only pulling out the hose and bringing it to the cars; I also taught him how to rinse off the wheels for me.

I think Cycle was more of a perfectionist than I was. People who saw us couldn't believe it, this 120-pound Rottweiler spraying a limousine's wheels with water over and over again. During our year and a half together, I taught Cycle all sorts of behaviors and tricks, both useful and silly. This dog had found his calling, and he couldn't get enough.

Ross came to graciously accept the new role I had created for Cycle. While it wasn't what he had originally wanted for his Rottweiler, he respected my opinion about dogs and adjusted to the new situation.

Cycle never did end up doing personal protection work for Ross. He was top-notch at alerting his owner to danger, and he could play the part of a scary, barking Rottweiler to perfection. But he wasn't an attack dog at heart. He never excelled at it because he just wasn't being his authentic self. To have success as a trainer—and more important, to nurture a happy, emotionally balanced dog—you have to work with the energy you have. You have to let your dog be *authentic*.

From working with Cycle, I learned to trust my intuition about a dog and to never force him to go against his authentic self. That would become a major part of the foundation of my rehabilitation methods.

It would take a little longer for me to be able to apply that lesson about authenticity to myself.

But above all, in order to be, never try to seem.
—Albert Camus

How Dogs Are Authentic

- Dogs are born with a certain energy that remains with them for life. It's not something that can be changed or faked.

- Dogs don't lie. With their energy and body language, they are always telling us exactly what they are thinking and feeling at any moment.

- Dogs are incredibly attuned to authenticity in humans. They can read your energy and discern your intent instantly.

- Dogs are entirely honest with one another. They know right away if another dog is going to be a friend, a foe, or an acquaintance. They instantly express who they are and what they want.

- Dogs are authentic by nature, and authenticity is crucial to their state of balance and well-being. They instinctively know what they are meant to do — they just need humans to allow them to do it.

Raising Cain

Cain was anybody's ideal Rottweiler: the entire package. His head was huge and square-jawed and his piercing eyes fixed on you with intensity. His body was lean but heavily muscled, his coat was a gleaming brown-black, and his posture would put any American Kennel Club dog to shame.

I nicknamed Cain the Chairman of the Board, after Frank Sinatra. It wasn't just his deep blue eyes that reminded me of the celebrated crooner; Cain was born with a formidable charisma. When he walked into a room, everybody sensed it. And like Sinatra, Cain never had to overdo it; he had grace and class. His powerful energy was understated, refined, but absolutely undeniable.

Cain came to me after I had finally hung out my own shingle. Ross had sold his business after I'd been with him for a year and a half, but he told me I should talk with the new owner because "we needed each other." The new owner, a guy named Waldo, told me he wanted protection for his warehouse in South L.A. He said the gang members were afraid of large, powerful breed dogs like mine and wanted me to patrol the warehouse with them every night. In exchange, he said I could have the huge, fenced-in parking lot next door as a place to work with dogs. Ross was right: It was a perfect arrangement.

By that point, I had saved up approximately $15,000 from a year and a half of nonstop work washing limos and training dogs—more than enough money to start my own business. I went to L.A. City Hall and purchased a business license for about $200, and that was the extent of my start-up costs.

I named my new business the Dog Psychology Center for a reason. By that point in my life, I knew I didn't want to be a traditional dog trainer, because I didn't think dog *training*—like the kind of work they did at All-American Dog Training Academy—actually addressed the problems facing dogs and their owners in my adopted country.

Deep in my heart, I believed that Americans didn't understand what their dogs needed to be happy. But I'd seen from the successes I'd already had with my clients that loving dog owners were willing and able to learn. I was doing a lot of reading at that time, trying to find any kind of backup for my theories, and happened upon a book called *Dog Psychology: The Basis of Dog Training*. The author, Dr. Leon F.

Whitney, is a world-renowned, London-based veterinarian who intellectually described everything I had come to know instinctually. Dr. Whitney—whom I was honored to meet and thank personally in Cannes, France, many years later— was the inspiration for the name of my new business.

My friends and even my ex-wife thought I was crazy. "No one will know what a dog psychology center is," they said. But I persisted, because I knew in my heart that the name was right. And in this case, being authentic served me well.

The original Dog Psychology Center consisted of a fenced-off lot and small warehouse in the industrial district of South L.A. It wasn't much, and it was in a rough neighborhood. But it was the right size, the rent was affordable, and it was mine. Word was already out that I was good with aggressive dogs — and now, people had a consistent place to come and find me.

Cain's owner, NFL linebacker Roman Phifer—at the time, a player for the original Los Angeles Rams—was one of my first big clients. In the power and charisma departments, Roman was pretty impressive himself. When we met, he was six feet two inches tall and a lean 237 pounds, and he could bench-press 380. He was also incredibly intelligent. Sports-writers described the way he operated on the field as a "finesse" game—but he had no idea how to finesse his relationship with his dog.

"Help me, man," he said when he showed up at the center with his two beautiful dogs in tow. Pointing to Cain, he told me, "My dog is attacking my friends!"

As with many of my clients, Roman's problem had to do with the dynamics in his household. Remember, when people first bring dogs into their lives, they don't always know what to do with them—and this is especially the case with

Can you tell by my face that I really enjoy my job? We can learn a lot about giving and receiving love by the way dogs treat us.

powerful breeds. Of course, they choose these breeds because they're big, they're beautiful, and they reflect a certain kind of image. But owners sometimes have an expectation that their new pet will be perfect right out of the gate, without understanding what a particular animal needs to be balanced and fulfilled.

When Roman brought him to me, Cain was an adolescent, which is the trickiest time in a dog's development. As with human adolescence, it's a phase of testing and pushing the limits — and, for the first time, discerning the limitations in the human owner.

Roman was young and single and hung out a lot at his house with other young, single players from his team. Being a strong male himself, he automatically assumed Cain would defer to him and his equally macho friends. But Cain knew his own power better than his owner did. He wasn't going to be anyone's pretty, obedient mascot.

Turns out that a couple of Roman's best friends were hiding a secret fear of dogs — especially of powerful breed dogs like Rotties. They covered it up, of course, but Cain sensed it right off the bat. All the testosterone- and adrenaline-charged male energy generated by Roman and his buddies was making Cain even more powerful, and he was determined to assert his place as an equal in Roman's circle. When Roman's friends would try to act tough around him, Cain would show them that he knew their secret by growling and biting. He was saying to the group, "Don't underestimate me. I was born to be one of you guys."

Over My Head

Roman was in way over his head with Cain, so after about a year in his household, he left him with me at the center. What nobody knew at the time was that I was in over my head as well.

It was 1994 and I had just married my 19-year-old girlfriend after learning she was pregnant. We'd only been dating for 10 months and didn't know each other that well. At age 24, I definitely hadn't been planning on settling down so soon. However, I was raised by my parents to be honorable when it comes to women, and I wanted to do the right thing.

No sooner was the wedding over than I realized that I was completely unprepared for marriage and a baby. At the time, I didn't even have a checking account. I was living with six dogs in a converted studio in a friend's backyard and was putting almost all my extra money into my new business, which wasn't yet turning a profit. I was charging only $10 a day to board and train each dog. Even though there were between 15 to 50 dogs on board at any given time, not even half of those were from paying clients who wanted me to fix behavior problems. The rest of my dogs were strays that I took in from rescue groups or found in the streets myself.

I also didn't have any relatives in America, so my only connection to family came from my wife's parents and brothers, who were of Latin descent but had adopted American values. I had no clue how to integrate the rigid gender roles of my native country with what my very American wife expected.

When my son Andre was born and I was suddenly a new dad, I became even more confused. I wanted to be respected, but I had muddled up the notion of respect with fear. Like Roman's football player friends, I had a lot of secret fears that I wanted to hide. I desperately looked around for some sort of role model who might help me become the man I wanted to be.

> *When I look around, I always learn something*
> *and that is to be always yourself ... Do not go out and look*
> *for a successful personality and try to duplicate it.*
> —Bruce Lee

Wearing the Wrong Mask

One day during this period of my life—my mid-20s—I saw that the movie *Scarface* was playing on TV. I'd heard a lot about it from my friends and decided to tune in. The main character—a cocaine dealer named Tony Montana, played by Al Pacino—mesmerized me. He reminded me of the powerful, macho figures I'd come to know while growing up—the El Chapo–style drug lord. In our working-class neighborhood in Mazatlán, we were in proximity to crime all the time. At school, many of my classmates idolized the power of the rich kingpins who flaunted their wealth and controlled the city through fear.

Now, living and working in South Central L.A., my next-door neighbors were members of the African-American and Hispanic gangs that ruled the streets in the 1990s. That was the definition of power I saw around me back then—all day, every day.

Al Pacino is a compelling actor, and his performance brought Tony Montana to life. There were no limits to what this character wanted to accomplish. I, too, had big dreams, and that quality appealed to me. Tony also had absolutely no fear. I urgently wanted to be fearless in pursuit of my dreams—even as I was secretly terrified in my new role as husband and father.

So I made the impulsive decision to act fearless and ruthless, like Tony. Never mind that his outward behavior in no way reflects my true nature. Adopting Tony's persona was a way to protect myself from the insecurity I felt inside.

But I took my inspiration to extremes. I began to talk like Tony, mimicking his style. At the time, I was paying cash to a local teenager named Andreas to help me out at the center in the afternoons, and from time to time I'd hire his little brother to help out, too. Both of them were shocked to watch me transform from a naturally quiet, reasonable boss into a demanding, obnoxious tyrant. I also became bellicose and demanding at home. My new wife didn't know what was going on with me, and she didn't like it one bit. To be perfectly honest, I can't say that I liked it either. But having a mask to cover my insecurities was a relief—and at the time, it felt like some sort of solution.

Never Lie to a Dog

It wasn't long before my macho Tony Montana act started hurting me in all areas of my life. Before I'd taken on this persona, things had been fine; I'd had no direct contact with the gangs that ran the streets where my Dog Psychology Center was located, and we had coexisted peacefully. In fact, they respected me because I would walk and rollerblade through the streets, accompanied by a pack of powerful dogs in perfect alignment.

Local business owners had also noticed me around town, and actually started paying me to ensure that I'd patrol their properties every night with my dogs. (I thought they were crazy, because I was walking the dogs by all those warehouses and parking lots anyway. But I took the money gladly!) As a result of these nightly walks, the alleys and streets became cleaner. After 6 p.m., locals had gotten into the habit of dumping their trash, old furniture, and other junk in the alleyways; once word spread that there were powerful dogs patrolling the area, the people stopped dumping trash.

The gang members didn't know how I could handle all these dogs—often, all off-leash. It symbolized power to them, so they left me alone. But after my transformation into Tony Montana, I started acting like a gangster myself. I'd walk with a swagger. I changed the way I dressed, going from wearing regular casual work clothes to the kind of flashy

Miami gangster duds that Al Pacino wears in the movie. I'd even started mouthing off to the gang members I ran into, bordering on the kind of disrespect that they weren't about to tolerate for long. Looking back, I can't believe the kind of stupid risks I was taking with my tough-guy act. But at the time, I really thought I was pulling it off.

The dogs in my pack at the Dog Psychology Center were the ones that busted up my Tony Montana act. I was training six huge Rottweilers (including Cain), along with my pit bull Daddy, who was then just a puppy. Until now, the whole "secret" behind my "dog whispering" skills was my calm, assertive energy. Animals naturally respect this kind of energy, and when they respect you, they will listen to and follow you. But assertive does not mean aggressive! And my Tony Montana persona was super-aggressive. That kind of energy is perceived by animals as unstable—and as I've always said, humans are the only animals who will follow an unstable leader.

Cain was the most dominant dog in the pack, and he was the one who saw through me first. When I would swagger around, he would do two things: first, mimic my arrogant energy; and second, usurp my leadership position by disobeying me (when the other dogs saw him disobeying, they'd rebel too). For Cain, my Tony Montana behavior was yet another challenge by a guy who was acting tough and macho but was insecure underneath. And since I, as the human leader, was acting unstable, he simply took over the pack.

Any team that has two leaders giving completely different instructions will eventually dissolve into chaos, and that's what happened with my pack. They had Cain and they had me—and between the two of us, only Cain really knew who he was. When I went out for pack walks, they would scatter all over the place.

I was young and confused, and at first I didn't realize what was wrong. But when I started losing control of the dogs, the gangsters in the neighborhood didn't look on me with respect anymore. Because I was dressing like a drug dealer and walking around like I owned the streets, I was making myself a target.

One day, I was with a friend who'd known me since I came to Los Angeles. Observing my behavior and how I'd changed, he asked, "What's wrong with you? Who do you think you

 FROM THE SCIENCE FILES

Fool a Dog, Lose Her Trust

In a 2015 issue of the peer-reviewed journal *Animal Cognition,* there's a study by scientists from Japan's Kyoto University that strongly suggests that people who deceive their dogs risk losing their dogs' trust in the long term.[6]

The Japanese researchers first laid out two sealed, opaque containers: one containing food, the other empty. In round one of the study, the researchers indicated clearly which was the food-bearing container before letting the dogs go find the treat. In round two, the experimenters purposely deceived the dogs by pointing them toward the empty container. Finally, the same experimenters pointed to the food-filled bin, just as they had in round one—with dramatically different results. The second time around, only 8 percent of the dogs followed the humans' directions.

The study concluded that dogs are keenly aware of humans who give them unreliable information. In other words, fool a dog once, shame on the dog. Fool a dog twice, shame on you, because she may never trust you again.

are?" I looked at him, confused. "If you continue to act this way, you're either going to get shot, or you're going to lose control of all those dogs someday," he said soberly.

In that moment, the light went on and I realized that the dogs' unpredictable behavior was triggered by my own inauthenticity. They no longer took me seriously, and would no longer follow me. In the animal world, pack leaders can't be inauthentic, which is a clear sign of instability. Dogs may tolerate it, but they won't buy it.

Killing Off Tony Montana

For me, Tony Montana was the wrong solution to a real problem. When faced with a situation that confounded me and made me feel insecure and afraid, I chose an inauthentic persona—based, of all things, on a fictional movie character—to hide behind. Ironically, that immature choice, which I made to protect myself, could have permanently ruined my relationships with my dogs—and damaged my fledgling business.

My natural skills with dogs are and always have been completely dependent on my authenticity and total honesty with the animals I'm working with. To do what I do requires a calm, assertive energy that comes from the core; it's never a part that I play. If I'd continued along that artificial path, I would not have been able to consistently help dogs, and eventually, my business would probably have floundered. Without knowing it, I almost sabotaged my own life's dream by not owning up to my fears and weakness or moving through them in order to grow.

What Cain taught me was that being myself was good enough—even if that "self" wasn't always confident of his place in the human world. Dogs are patient enough to let you work through your human issues — as long as you're not projecting a dishonest or an unstable energy when you interact with them. Dogs expect nothing but honesty. They deserve nothing but authenticity. And to become more authentic, we must often unlearn a lot of what we think it takes to "succeed" in the human world. The best answer is always to reconnect with our basic, most honest and honorable instincts.

In order to kill off Tony Montana for good, I took a photo of myself. Then I took a photo of Al Pacino as Tony Montana and pasted my face over his. I keep it in my home to this day, to remind me of the time when I wasn't being authentic.

Re-raising Cain

It turned out that Cain knew exactly who he was and what he was born to be all along; he didn't need fixing after all. It was his owner and I who did.

In response, I adjusted my attitude and made a vow to always be true to myself and my dogs. This helped me mend my relationship with Cain. We established a rich new bond by engaging in more playful, lighthearted activities together. We would go to the beach above Malibu and play fetch in new and natural surroundings. We would run together in the hills and splash together in the bracing ocean waves. We did all sorts of fun, silly, joyful things together designed to bring out his playful side and reestablish his trust in me: the opposite of activities that would trigger his dominance.

Next, I worked with Cain's owner, Roman, to help him establish a calm-assertive leadership style with his dog. I

From the Celebrity Files

Alec and Hilaria Baldwin

My client Alec Baldwin is known as one of the busiest, most diligent actors working today. His full-time job is to create characters and wear masks. Out on the street, he's got a larger-than-life reputation as a guy who isn't afraid to speak his mind, which can make a lot of people angry. He finds that one-dimensional image frustratingly hard to shake.

"Alec is not well understood by many people," says his wife, Hilaria, a well-known Manhattan yoga instructor. "When he walks down the street, he is extremely noticeable. All the recognition can be exhausting, especially living in a busy place like New York. He can't go anywhere and hide. His public life is so chaotic. But what we love about our dogs is that they have no idea that he's famous. They love him unconditionally as much as he loves them unconditionally. It's a really pure relationship—probably one of the purest he'll ever have."

Alec's dogs know exactly who he is, in his heart and soul. They don't see the guy who wears the masks, or even the controversial guy who can sometimes abrasively speak his mind on the news or in the tabloids. Alec's dogs are well behaved and balanced because he shares only his authentic self with them. In turn, they reflect back to him a side of himself that the public doesn't often see.

Dogs give us the priceless gift of being able to relax and be true to our authentic selves, flaws and all—and to be loved unconditionally anyway.

taught Roman how to immediately recognize when Cain was uncomfortable with someone (particularly his dog-phobic friends who were projecting bravado but feeling fear).

Two years later, Roman got married, and I worked with him and Cain to help convince his new wife that Cain would be safe and reliable around their new baby. Several years later, after Roman got divorced, he contacted me again to help Cain forge a healthy relationship with his new girlfriend and her tiny Chihuahua.

Cain's happy ending? He was never aggressive toward Roman's friends again. In fact, Roman and his family brought Cain with them everywhere they traveled; he became a trusted family member and a canine "big brother" to his kids.

I will never forget that remarkable Rottweiler and the vital lesson about building self-confidence that he taught me.

The Four Worlds

I've transformed many of the things I've learned from dogs into simple concepts that can be easily taught and digested. One of these concepts relates directly to the idea of authenticity and centers on what I call "the four worlds."

I believe human existence is made up of four very different ways of perceiving and moving through our lives' events and our interactions with others. They are:

The spiritual world
The emotional world
The intellectual world
The instinctual world

To show you what I mean, here are a few examples. A priest might live mostly in the spiritual world, while a data analyst might primarily inhabit the intellectual world. A romance novelist would live in the intellectual and emotional worlds, while a farmer might inhabit the instinctual world most of the time.

We can move between worlds depending on our environment or circumstance. For example, a lawyer who moves primarily in the intellectual realm at work may return to an emotional realm when she comes home to her kids. But most people gravitate toward one dominant world.

If you remember anything, remember this: *Whichever of the four worlds you are living in at any given moment provides the lens through which you view life and defines your reality.* In turn, that reality will shape the way you relate to all other people, animals, and things. It also determines how you will respond to any situation in any given moment.

If you are mostly in the intellectual world and interacting with a person who is firmly in the emotional world, you could appear to them to lack compassion or empathy. If you are in the spiritual world and interacting with someone in the intellectual world, you could appear superstitious or irrational. Acknowledging these four worlds and identifying which one we're in at any given time helps us better communicate with and understand one another. And increasing and improving communication always increases authenticity.

While most humans usually reside somewhere on the continuum between the intellectual and emotional realms, dogs—like all other animals—are permanent residents of the instinctual world. I am always firmly in the instinctual world when I work with a troubled dog, so I can relate to him on his level.

Recollect that the Almighty, who gave the dog to be companion of our pleasures and our toils, hath invested him with a nature noble and incapable of deceit.
— Sir Walter Scott

Humans May Lie, But Dogs Never Do

When I am called in to assess a client's problem dog, I usually sit down and listen to my client anxiously tell me a long, detailed story of how his dog is misbehaving and why. But in my experience, the cause of the misbehavior is almost never what the dog owner has described.

Of course, I listen intently and observe the emotion and drama the dog's owner injects into the story, which has clearly become an important part of the narrative. Then I look at the dog. He will tell me, "My owner is emotionally unbalanced, and I'm fearful." Or "My owner ignores me and I'm bored. That's why I am tearing up the furniture." Dogs instantly tell me what's really going on in their house, and what is really happening with their owners. That's why I always say, humans tell me the story, but dogs tell me the truth.

Reconnect With Your Instinctual Self

A dog's instincts are not premeditated. When a dog bites, it's because he's feeling fearful or challenged, not because he doesn't like you or was offended by something you said. Dogs act instinctually, which means they act authentically. If we use dogs as our examples, we can take the first steps toward becoming more authentic.

 ## Dog Lesson #4
How to Be Authentic

- ✅ Be aware of your instincts, remembering that your first reaction or response is usually the most authentic. (It may not always be the right reaction, but it will always be the most authentic one.)

- ✅ Observe the body language of others. The body rarely lies (especially the eyes).

- ✅ Be wary of the times your inner voice warns you of the possible consequences of telling the truth. Your inner voice will say, "I can't say that because I might lose my job." Or "I can't tell him that because he will never understand." Challenge these assumptions, because they're often wrong, and they always make us less authentic.

LESSON 5:
FORGIVENESS

Dogs, for a reason that can only be described as divine, have the ability to forgive, let go of the past, and live each day joyously. It's something the rest of us strive for.
—Jennifer Skiff, *The Divinity of Dogs*

The witnesses would say later that they heard the yelping first: the unbearable, agonizing wails of an innocent animal in excruciating pain. They were the kinds of sounds that stop the hearts of compassionate people everywhere.

The cries came closer and closer. In the gritty, working-class neighborhood of South Central L.A., more people came to their windows. Several came out to the street to see what was happening.

Then, hurtling down the street came the ball of fire. A blaze of flames, the sickening smell of gasoline and burning flesh, and underneath, the dog, running down the street toward them, her mouth open, her eyes rounded by terror.

It was sickeningly obvious: Someone had set this pit bull on fire.

Among the witnesses there were a few Good Samaritans who rushed to the poor dog's aid, throwing a blanket over the flames, bringing cold, wet towels, and calming her down until animal control could arrive. She made it alive to a nearby animal hospital, where the emergency vets rushed to tend to the raw and ugly third-degree burns that ran all the way down her muscular back.

Weeks later, Hearts and Tails, a small but passionate rescue group, liberated the pit bull from the hospital and took her in. Her saviors named her Rosemary.

Rosemary was a delicate white-and-tan pit bull mix who'd been ejected from an illegal dog-fighting ring. We never learned how or why she had been set on fire, but it was without a doubt done deliberately. Maybe she had angered her captors. Maybe she'd lost an important fight and they decided they were through with her. But more likely—since Rosemary was a small, gentle soul—she was probably used as a bait dog to teach the other dog fighters how to kill. Perhaps her tormentors weren't angry at all, but just feeling a little more sadistic than usual that day. Whatever the reason—can there ever be a reason for something so barbaric?—they'd poured gasoline all over her beautiful back, lit a match, and then laughed as she ran down a South Central L.A. street, orange flames leaping from her as she howled in pain and betrayal.

Thank God there are groups of rescuers out there who, like me, believe that no animal—no matter how damaged by nature, accident, or humans—ever deserves to be thrown away. These people are the most compassionate souls on

Earth—and also the strongest, because they have seen at close range the way people abuse, neglect, and even torture dogs. It's the worst of human nature on display, every day. When you see what a human being is capable of doing to an innocent, helpless animal, it diminishes your trust in the entire race.

The good people of Hearts and Tails paid Rosemary's hospital bills by collecting donations during the time she was in intensive treatment for her burns. After she had begun to heal, she was released from the hospital and brought to a foster home, where she could begin her long-term physical and psychological recovery. But soon, it began to look as if not only her body but also her heart had been permanently scarred by humans.

Rosemary began showing aggression almost immediately, snarling and snapping at some of the rescue workers who were trying to help her. While on a walk with the woman who was fostering her, she attacked two elderly men. If she hadn't been in the company of experienced, dedicated rescuers, she surely would have been put down. But they knew what she'd survived, and they wanted to give her one more chance to have the life she deserved. They brought her to me as her last chance of hope.

Rosemary would teach me a profound lesson in forgiveness that still affects me to this day.

The people that set one animal against another haven't the guts to be bullies themselves. They're just secondhand cowards.
—Cleveland Amory

Rebuilding Trust

Rosemary was described to me as a deadly, dangerous dog, but I recognized right away that her aggression was 100 percent based in fear. She was a low-energy, back-of-the-pack dog at heart, with no desire at all to fight (which might have been why she was rejected by her dog-fighting owners). Examining her scarred body, I saw that she had not been used as a breeding dog, because she hadn't had puppies. Dog fighters generally look for more dominant females to use for breeding.

As I do with all dogs, I let Rosemary become accustomed to me on her own terms. I separated her from the rest of my pack for the first few days and just sat by her silently for long periods of time, waiting for her to approach me when she was ready. The first time she came to me, she licked my face, then sighed and laid her head in my lap. It became apparent that the real Rosemary was naturally gentle and incredibly affectionate. She had been attacking people because that's what she had become accustomed to. In her dog-fighting past, she associated humans with pain and abuse, so she'd strike first defensively. She'd get them before they could hurt her.

Being around the rest of my pack—which at that time had grown to about 40 or 50 dogs—helped Rosemary's heart heal, too. Dogs don't care if another dog is scarred by burns, or missing an eye or a leg. They read only that dog's energy—and Rosemary, though shy at first, had a warm, tender way that they immediately welcomed.

As Rosemary spent more and more time in the accepting company of the dogs of my pack, my wife and kids, and the loving humans at the Dog Psychology Center, she began to come out of her shell. I instructed all visitors to the center

One way to teach dogs trust and respect is by introducing them
to a pack, where they can find their place within the group.

to approach her respectfully, giving her space as well as following my rules for meeting any dog: No touch, no talk, no eye contact at first.

Watching Rosemary build trust and affection with humans for the first time in her life was truly a spiritual experience for me. Her ability to forgive was close to divine. Here was a dog that had experienced a lifetime of the most extreme abuse imaginable at the hands of humans—and yet she had gone from defensively attacking the rescue workers to lovingly nuzzling my young sons, Calvin and Andre, as they played with the dogs at the center after school.

To err is human—to forgive, canine.
—Unknown

★ FROM THE CELEBRITY FILES

Kesha

Singer, songwriter, rapper, and actor Kesha (full name Kesha Rose Seber) has a love and respect for all animals that runs deep. As the first global ambassador for the Humane Society of the United States, she has campaigned against animal testing worldwide. She's helped rescue hundreds of animals in her young life, many of which have been victims of abandonment, abuse, or neglect. And so she's seen their extraordinary ability to forgive up close.

"Dogs just trust you. It's so unconditional and pure and beautiful," Kesha says. "I feel like my soul, when I started this life, was just like that. But over the years, it's hard not to become jaded. And you think that the spirit of animals is something to strive for because it's just so beautiful and pure—and that's what I always try to bring myself back to."

Recently, Kesha herself has faced adversity during a public two-year legal battle with her former record producer. In 2016, the singer filed to dismiss the lawsuit in order to move forward with her career. Watching dogs move on and flourish after enduring unimaginable abuse or neglect has been an inspiration for the artist in how to overcome the many setbacks and betrayals in her own life.

Rosemary Finds Her Purpose

Rosemary had even more to offer the pack than just her growing ability to trust. Throughout nature—in whales, primates, and especially wolves—every animal has its place.

In fact, many species' survival depends on a tradition of "single mothers" or older females playing "nanny" to the newly born generation. It turned out that Rosemary was born to be such a nanny.

Around this time—only about two years after I opened the Dog Psychology Center—people in our South Central L.A. neighborhood had started treating us as if we were an animal shelter. They'd drop off pregnant dogs or boxes full of abandoned puppies at our gate. We never refused any of them; we rehabilitated the ones with behavior issues and later contacted one of the many rescue organizations we worked with to help us find them good homes.

The very first time Rosemary saw me carrying in a box of tiny puppies, she came alive inside. From then on, she and those puppies were inseparable. If the puppies were so small that we had to feed them with a dropper, she'd be right there to lick them afterward. If they needed a mother figure to snuggle with at night, Rosemary would offer up the warmth of her scarred body to keep them safe.

Whenever a pregnant mom or orphaned puppies joined our pack temporarily, Rosemary became their official nanny. She had an endless supply of tenderness and affection. She was also a terrific disciplinarian. Puppies need firm boundaries and limitations, which they learn from their mothers. It's also how they learn canine social skills (which, by the way, is why so many puppy-mill dogs have behavioral problems). The mothers at puppy mills are breeding machines, and are usually so stressed and abused from a lifetime of what amounts to torture that they can't parent properly. Their puppies never learn how to be dogs. Rosemary made sure that all the puppies that passed

Michael Vick's Fighting Dogs

I n early April 2007, a convoy of federal agents and local law enforcement officials descended on a 15-acre Virginia property. Known as the Bad News Kennels, it was owned by Atlanta Falcons quarterback Michael Vick. Inside, they discovered evidence of a multimillion-dollar underground dog-fighting ring. They confiscated nearly 70 captive dogs, mostly pit bulls. Many were gravely injured.

Michael Vick pleaded guilty and went to jail—but what would happen to the liberated pit bulls? Even the ASPCA's policy was that all fighting dogs must be put down. A team of dedicated and passionate volunteers was going to make sure that that didn't happen.

through the Dog Psychology Center left with Ph.D.'s in canine sociability!

Rosemary's gentle, loving spirit and her ability to forgive and move on have been an inspiration to every human who has ever met her—and to many who have simply heard her story.

Popeye

Popeye and Rosemary were members of my pack at around the same time. Popeye, a sinewy, purebred red-nosed pit

In his book *The Lost Dogs: Michael Vick's Dogs and Their Tale of Rescue and Redemption*, author Jim Gorant follows the story of the rescue and redemption of Vick's canine victims. A panel of experts evaluated the behavior of the 49 rescued dogs and found that 16 could go directly to foster homes to await adoption. Two were suitable for police work, and 30 were sent to a sanctuary—a place where dogs deemed unsafe for adoption are allowed to live out the remainder of their lives in a pleasant environment while being fed and nurtured by caring humans. Only one dog—a female who had been forcibly bred to the point where she'd gone mad with aggression—had to be euthanized.

Eight years later, everyone who adopted the dogs still marvels at their pets' ability to overcome their pasts—and their unique capacity for love. What an astonishing example of a dog's willingness to forgive.

bull, was another victim of the dog-fighting industry. He was found after being discarded by his captors on the street. He had just lost an eye in a fight, and when the socket healed, he was left with a rakish, pirate-like appearance. While Popeye was adjusting to his strange, new one-eyed perspective on the world, he became suspicious of other dogs and acted aggressively toward them to cover up his vulnerability. When his aggression extended to people, the rescue workers who'd saved him brought him to me.

Unlike Rosemary, Popeye had been bred to fight, so his previous owners had encouraged the dominant, aggressive side of his nature. He was a high-strung, dominant guy when he first came to us, with an alpha dog's instincts and a powerful energy that could turn dangerous when he felt threatened (which, at the beginning, was all the time). When I first started working with him, I had to be on high alert in case he'd feel insecure for some reason and strike out. But as it had with Rosemary, the mellow, sociable, highly structured environment of the pack eventually calmed him down, along with the constant exposure to respectful humans who wanted to help him heal. After about six months, he integrated smoothly into his new life at the Dog Psychology Center and was never aggressive toward humans again.

Dogs show us an infinite ability to forgive. I think their power of forgiveness is related to living in the moment. They don't carry things with them, which is an important lesson for us.
—Dr. Andrew Weil

You Are *Not* Your Story

Both Rosemary and Popeye became iconic dogs at the Dog Psychology Center and made cameos in many of the early *Dog Whisperer* episodes. That's because their physical defects made them stand out from the other dogs in the pack. People would see Rosemary's scars and Popeye's eye and ask, "Oooh, what happened to them?" Despite everyone's burning curiosity, I felt uncomfortable telling their sad stories over and over again.

*Popeye was an inspiration for everyone at the Dog Psychology Center—
he was able to overcome his injury and trust humans again.*

That's because one of the most important lessons dogs can teach us about forgiveness is that *you are not your story.* Dogs don't hold on to the past the way we do. Memories can be precious, but if replaying incidents from our lives that we'd be better off forgetting keeps us from truly appreciating the moment or moving forward, we need to take a deep breath—and look to dogs like Rosemary and Popeye as inspiring examples.

Many of my clients are overly preoccupied with their dogs' pasts—much more, in fact, than the dogs themselves are. Especially if they have adopted rescue dogs or abuse victims, owners will often make up their own creative stories about what *might* have happened to a dog before she came into their life. "She must've been kicked a lot, because she's afraid of boots." "He won't get into the van—I think he might have been thrown out of one!" Even when a story of neglect or abuse is true, owners unwittingly hold their dogs back from overcoming their pasts by generating too much negative energy.

Stay in the Present

Rosemary, who suffered the most horrendous cruelty and abuse imaginable, was able to move forward and forgive the species that had hurt her. With Popeye, who was raised to hate and attack, it took a little longer—but eventually, he also accepted a completely new way of living. That's because dogs, when given the opportunity, will *always* move toward balance. They don't want to spend their lives psychologically handicapped or tied to an event that is far behind them. Dogs are meant to live in the moment, and that's what they prefer to do.

In my experience, it's humans who create imbalance in dogs, and humans who hold them back from being their best selves. It's not fair and it's not right—and it's one of the main motivations for me to continue to teach and spread this message: Learn to let go. If you can't do it for yourself, then, please, do it for your dog.

Holding On to Hurt

Can you imagine the reaction of a person who had undergone the kind of trauma that Rosemary suffered? There are millions of human victims out there who have also suffered abuse, rejection, injustice, and violence. For most, it takes years of healing, struggle, and therapy to be able to put the past in its place; many never succeed in moving forward and working through their pain. Part of this is because we humans are blessed and cursed with powerful, visceral, even cinematic memories. But it's also true that many humans become so comfortable in their pain and so identified with their role as a victim that they cling to past trauma, even when given the opportunity to let it go. What can we learn from dogs that can help us cope when the unthinkable happens?

How Dogs Forgive

- ✅ Dogs can't assign abstract meaning to events in their lives. They can only make associations related to those experiences.

- ✅ Dogs can form new, positive associations with past events and move forward if given the opportunity.

- ✅ Dogs are wired to experience every moment, which allows them to fully appreciate the now.

- ✅ Dogs are free to let go of past traumas that might otherwise hold them back by living in a state where the now is the only thing that matters.

I am with a pack of dogs nearly every day of my life, so their influence on me is profound. Whether I am running with the pack through the Santa Clarita hills, throwing a ball with them on the Malibu beach, or working with a client to help his troubled dog find balance, I'm blessed to be able to spend most of my time in the moment—the way all dogs do.

However, I'm only human, and like many others, I still struggle with holding on to resentments, remembering past trauma, and letting go of old business. Those of us who have managed to completely let go of past hurt, loss, and betrayal are incredibly enlightened, and I admire the hard work involved in reaching that spiritual level. It's what I strive for in my life—but I've learned the hard way that forgiveness is a journey, and there are often unseen bumps along its roads.

My dogs forgive ... the anger in me, the arrogance in me, the brute in me. They forgive everything I do before I forgive myself.
—Guy de la Valdéne, *For a Handful of Feathers*

A Journey Into Darkness

After years of struggle, I was blessed: The dream that I had come to America to fulfill suddenly came true beyond my wildest imagination. Along the way, it had shifted and developed into a new mission, unique to my talents and everything I'd discovered about America's dogs and myself since that first day with Daisy in Chula Vista Grooming Parlor. Instead of being the "best dog trainer in the world," as I'd hoped to be, I was now more of a people trainer. In the process of rehabilitating problem dogs, I'd learned that teaching owners to understand what dogs were trying to say with their behavior was the key to helping both animals and humans have better lives.

In 2004, my first television series, *Dog Whisperer With Cesar Millan,* launched on National Geographic Channel; and in 2006 my first book, *Cesar's Way,* was published. *Dog Whisperer* went on to air for nine seasons, and *Cesar's Way* became an international bestseller.

Sometimes, I look back on those years and picture a tornado like the one in the movie *The Wizard of Oz.* Flying around inside it are hundreds of magical things: the excitement of being able to move my wife and two sons from our tiny rented home in the L.A. hood of Inglewood into a beautiful new home in Santa Clarita; having my show recognized by the Emmys and the People's Choice Awards; watching my books hit the *New York Times* bestseller lists; and speaking in front of thousands of fans in venues all over the world.

But also inside that tornado were dark and dangerous elements: increasing work demands that interfered with precious family time; constant travel that kept me away from my boys; the frustration I felt at not being able to control certain aspects of my own business; the arguments I had with my wife as we struggled to navigate the exciting but stormy waters of a life that had transformed seemingly overnight.

Those years went by in a blur. Then, in April 2010, my wife floored me by telling me she was filing for divorce. It came as a complete shock. I was on location in Ireland, getting ready to perform my live show, when I received the call. I was fragile, sleep-deprived, and stressed-out over business issues that had come to a boiling point. I had to go on stage moments after I got the call—and ironically, it was the very best live show I've ever done. I've never been so full of raw emotion or vulnerability, before or since.

After I got off stage, the pain began to sink in. I felt angry and betrayed. I know I was far from perfect, but I felt I had been trying so hard. In fact, before my wife called to announce she was leaving, I had been excitedly awaiting her arrival in Europe with Calvin and Andre, who had never been overseas before.

For months, the prospect of a family vacation in an exciting new place I could never have dreamed of visiting 10 years earlier had been all that was getting me through a grueling work schedule. When that bubble burst, it nearly destroyed me.

After my wife dropped her bomb, I still had many more 14-hour days of filming left to finish, as well as the intensity of performing my live show to huge auditoriums all across the U.K. I don't know how I made it through without col-

It took a lot of self-growth and healing to overcome my depression, but I can thank my pack for standing by my side through it all.

lapsing, but I did. I must have been in a fog, numb, because I don't remember a lot of details of that time; I was just waiting for the trip to end.

When I finally made it home to California, I felt completely drained—mentally, physically, emotionally, and spiritually. Not long after, I discovered that our family finances—which should have been very comfortable and secure at that point—were in shambles. Next, it became clear that my longtime business partners had not been working in my best interests, and I learned that I'd lost control of my own business and my TV show. I had never felt so alone.

I have since learned that a depression like the one I experienced then is a black hole. When you are in it long enough, you can't see the light anymore, and it truly feels like there is no way to climb out.

It has taken six years and a lot of hard work—including rebuilding my business and taking full charge of my own career for the first time—to clamber back out of that hole. I feel so grateful that my family, close colleagues, friends, and of course my fans all united behind me to see me through it.

Looking back now, I feel that pain has made me a much wiser, stronger, and more compassionate person. Having gone to a dark place that many less fortunate don't ever return from, I feel deep and sincere empathy for the suffering people I might not have understood in the past. They say God doesn't give us any more than we can handle—so, reflecting on that period of my life, I think God must've thought I was a lot stronger than I believed I ever could be. I'm so grateful that He was right.

FROM THE SCIENCE FILES

Forgiving Can Save Your Life

Popeye and Rosemary were on to something: Forgiveness, as it turns out, is not just something preached by religious and spiritual leaders anymore. Instead, it's a serious prescription for lifelong good health based on decades of rigorous medical research. Recent studies have found that forgiving those who have wronged us lowers blood pressure, bolsters the immune system, improves sleep, and increases life span.[7] People who know how to let go of their grudges tend to be healthier and live longer and are generally more satisfied with their lives. They experience far less depression, anxiety, stress, anger, and hostility.

People who cling to their resentments, however, are more likely to experience severe depression and post-traumatic stress disorder. They are ill more often—particularly with cardiac issues—and they heal more slowly, among other negative health problems.

Suffering is not holding you. You are holding suffering.
—Osho

Journey to Forgiveness

I wish I had been able to forgive the people in my life as cleanly and completely as did Rosemary, Popeye, and all the other abused dogs I've helped over the years. I am still in awe of a dog's ability to let go of horrendous torment and give unconditional love to the species responsible for their torture. I try every day to be more like the dogs that have over-come cruelty far worse than anything I've ever suffered.

One of the first steps on any journey to forgiveness is to try to see a situation through another person's eyes. Dogs have no problem with this, because their inclination is always "pack first, individual last." They see the world through the lens of what is best for the pack. With humans, however, empathy can be a lot harder.

When I think back on my first marriage, I can accept now that we were pushing a stone uphill from the start. As I always say, "the energy is the energy," and my ex-wife and I had an energy crisis from day one. We both did our best, but we were never a compatible couple.

The very worst part of the experience was a long period during which my sons refused to speak to me. I'd never experienced a divorce or even a very bad breakup before, and I wasn't prepared for the fact that people—even your own children—can and often do feel pressured to choose sides.

With the success of *Dog Whisperer,* I worked long hours and had to travel a lot. So I wasn't there to see my sons go to their first dances, or to see Andre score his first soccer goal. I wasn't there for the nightly dinners or to guide my sons when they were facing problems. In my absence, both my sons grew closer to my wife. When she told me she wanted a divorce, I desperately wanted to be able to get back home from Europe to try to save my marriage and my family—but I couldn't because I was contractually obli-gated to finish the tour. So my sons never did get to hear from me or see the situation through my eyes until much later. I suppose it was natural that I'd end up the "bad guy" in their minds.

I am not saying that I did nothing wrong in the marriage. But I was so focused on making a good living and providing for my family that I missed a lot of important times with my boys. They were angry. I think they believed that if I had been a better father—if I'd been around more, if I had paid more attention to them and their mom—the divorce wouldn't have happened. No child wants to see his parents split up.

At the time, I felt abandoned by everyone I thought had cared for me. My sons were and are a big part of the reason I get up every morning, and to feel like I was losing their love and support was devastating.

Today, everything has changed. I am closer to both Andre and Calvin than I ever have been before. I can let the dark days of the rift between us go. Now that they are older and can see events with clearer eyes, they understand my point of view as well as their mother's, and have a more mature perspective on why the marriage ended. They have both forgiven their parents for not being perfect.

Since Andre and Calvin are also working with dogs and doing some television work themselves, they even finally realize that their old dad does have something important to teach them! I'm grateful that I get to spend so much more time with them now than I could when they were younger and my life was so out of balance.

Today, with my fiancée, Jahira, I've finally experienced what a truly equal, supportive relationship feels like. I have begun to look back on my marriage with less emotion, and with a better understanding of both my own unhappiness and my ex-wife's. I can see things from both points of view and start to let go of the past.

There are some painful events in my rearview mirror that I am still struggling to release. But I feel blessed and inspired when I am able to watch a dog move past trauma and, through forgiveness, achieve the peace and balance that he seeks. Little by little, day by day, the lessons that dogs like Rosemary and Popeye have instilled encourage me to move toward serenity and forgiveness in every area of my life.

 ## DOG LESSON #5
How to Embrace Forgiveness

- ✅ Try to view the pain of the past the way a dog does: as something that pales in comparison with the joys of the present moment.

- ✅ Remember that fostering resentment is like drinking poison and then waiting for the other person to die. Resentments hurt only the resenter. Forgiveness is a choice you can make.

- ✅ Try to develop empathy for people who may have wronged you. By seeing the world through their eyes, you may better understand their actions.

- ✅ Forgiveness is a gift you give yourself. Don't expect apologies or reparations from another person; they may never come. Take it upon yourself to release all negative elements from your life.

- Celebrate the moment of now in all its Technicolor glory. Use dogs as your role models—they truly know how to experience the intensity of living in their every waking moment.

LESSON 6:
WISDOM

The purpose of life is not to be happy.
It is to be useful, to be honorable,
to be compassionate, to have it
make some difference that you
have lived and lived well.

—Leo Rosten

Every one of us has a person in our lives who has helped make us a better human. Maybe it's the teacher who inspired us to love learning, the parent who guided us through a rocky adolescence, or the coach who helped build our self-confidence on the playing field. We call them idols, heroes, or role models. Whatever title we choose, these individuals hold special places in our minds, our hearts, and our memories. They are the forces who help shape us into the people we aspire to become.

For me, that special someone is Daddy, the gentle giant of a red-nosed pit bull who was my right-hand dog for 16 years. He was always by my side, rehabilitating unbalanced animals with me long before my television show came along. People have called Daddy my helper and my sidekick. But neither one of those words begins to do him justice. When it came to understanding troubled dogs, Daddy was the genuine "Dog Whisperer"—he was the real deal. I was just his disciple.

Daddy's ability to empathize with and help others—not just other dogs but also every human he ever came into contact with—is something I had never seen before, and have had yet to see again since. He is my hero because, even to this day, nearly seven years after his death, he continues to influence me both emotionally and spiritually. Daddy set the highest of bars for me to become as kind, balanced, tolerant, and ethical as he was.

Daddy was far more than a well-behaved dog. He wasn't just smart. He wasn't just gentle. I may sound like I'm exaggerating here, but to me and everyone who spent any significant time with him, Daddy was a spiritual teacher. To me, he was all the greatness of history's most inspiring leaders rolled up into one beautiful canine. Somehow, that burly little pit bull had been born possessing what seemed to me to be the wisdom of the ages.

Daddy showed me that love and loyalty that go beyond words are possible in this life. And he also taught me to aspire to a new and distant goal: the attainment of true wisdom.

Wisdom Goes Beyond Knowledge

Wisdom is a generic term, and is used in many different ways. The kind of wisdom that Daddy taught me extends far beyond the usual definitions of mere intelligence or a vast breadth of knowledge. Contrary to what many believe, being smart is not the same as being wise.

A smart person knows a lot of facts and is well versed in information. Being smart is a function of the intellectual self. But a truly wise person—whether "book smart" or not—relies on the deeper knowledge that comes from instinct and life experience. According to the dictionary, "wisdom" is "the power of discerning and judging properly as to what is true or right"—and it's that discernment and judgment that make all the difference.

Daddy fit that definition perfectly.

Wisdom is composed of many parts. I believe it consists of inborn characteristics, personal qualities, and habits, along with acquired life lessons. It can include factual or intellectual knowledge, but doesn't have to. What wisdom really requires is having life experiences—and more important, learning from them all, both good and bad. The ability to take one's setbacks and suffering and transform them into transcendent life lessons is where any true journey to wisdom begins.

Daddy and Pit Bull Prejudice

Daddy belonged to Reginald "Reggie" Noble, better known as Redman, the celebrated rapper, DJ, music producer, and actor who needed my help training the four-month-old puppy he'd adopted from a breeder. (Redman had originally named the puppy "L.A. Daddy," but I shortened it and the nickname stuck.) He invited me to come down to his South Central L.A. warehouse/headquarters one day early in 1995 for a meeting.

I remember the day vividly. We were on the set of one of Redman's music videos, and all around us was chaos: film crews moving huge pieces of equipment, stage crew members carrying props, assistant directors shouting orders, rappers and dancers rehearsing in every corner of the room. Sitting at the foot of Redman's chair and seemingly oblivious to the fracas was a stocky, reddish butterball of a pit bull: about 20 pounds, with freshly cropped ears and an oversize, blocky head.

Though I was impressed by Daddy's naturally calm energy amid all that turmoil and distraction, I could also sense in him a hesitance and a mild insecurity. Such a quality in a dog can be both a blessing and a curse. Healthy caution can help a dog remain safe, calm, and socially respectful. But too much insecurity can create either debilitating fearfulness or—far worse—fear-based aggression.

There are millions of conscientious dog owners out there, and Redman is a good example of one. A smart and thoughtful guy, he was determined to be a responsible guardian for Daddy—for the good of both society and his dog. He'd seen some of his friends and colleagues with poorly socialized pit bulls dragged into court for their dogs' bad behavior, and he didn't want that for himself, for his family, or, of course, for Daddy.

Redman wanted a dog that wouldn't ever hurt anyone, that would be nonaggressive and obedient, and that he could take anywhere with him without the fear of getting sued. His manager was also behind the scenes, nagging him about legal liability, should Daddy ever decide to bite someone.

Redman loved Daddy from the start. But he was also at the beginning of his stardom and about to embark on a series of long, grueling tours. While he was gone, he wanted Daddy to stay with me so that the puppy could begin intensive training.

I shook hands with Redman, gave him my number, and turned just in time to see Daddy give me a searching look with his cool green eyes. I felt a shiver go up my spine, as if I'd known him all my life. All I had to say was "Come on, Daddy," and he calmly followed me out the door and into what would become our long journey together.

For Daddy and me, it was the start of something incredible. I believe we were brought into each other's lives for a reason, creating a friendship and a soul-bond that will stay with me for as long as I live.

The Teacher Becomes the Student

At four months, Daddy was at the ideal age to start shaping his young mind. But make no mistake: He was born with a quality that no human could instill in him. From the start, he was a curious, eager, and receptive pupil, with just one potential weakness: He was uncertain of himself and a little cautious. As part of his training, I worked on building up Daddy's self-esteem by introducing him to new situations and challenges. We took trips alone and with the pack to many different locations — the beach, the mountains, and a crowded street fair. I completed a variety of training exercises with him, from simple obedience to personal protection work to games where he would try to identify a specific scent. With each new challenge, Daddy began to overcome his fears even more.

When I think back on my own life, it's been those times

that I've pushed myself—that I've dared to go outside my comfort zone, no matter how scared I was inside—that I really grew as a person. As the weeks passed, Daddy reflected that experience as he became more independent and self-assured, while our bond began to strengthen.

Dogs end their official "puppyhood" at 9 or 10 months of age and enter into a rebellious adolescence that lasts until they are about two years old. Once I got Daddy through his childish insecurities, he passed through a brief prideful phase, where he wouldn't back down from a challenge. This got him into a few minor scuffles with some of my Rottweilers that tested his bravado. I responded by showing him that the right thing to do was just walk away—to surrender to the situation and hold his pride in check.

While at first it was I who schooled Daddy in the basics of avoiding conflict, the way he absorbed those lessons took them to a whole new level. It wasn't long before I felt like I was the student and he was the teacher.

By the time he was two years old, Daddy would remain cool, calm, and aloof when other dogs would try to pick fights with him. When faced with conflict, he would just stand his ground or simply ignore the aggressor, turn his head, and walk away. He was like that cool kid in high school who won't even bother with the other students' petty disagreements. Even then, Daddy seemed to instinctually know how to diffuse tense situations by taking a step back and letting the air go out of the bellicosity balloon.

I remember one day when a new dog I'd brought into the pack at the Dog Psychology Center decided to challenge Daddy to a face-off. As I watched Daddy walk away as if the troublesome dog didn't even exist, I had a lightbulb moment

Daddy was an inspiration—so humble and wise, he was a calming force in my life. And he was the true "Dog Whisperer."

of my own. Suddenly, the deeper value of surrender became clear to me.

Surrender is often not just the most practical but also the most admirable choice. When you surrender, you avoid conflict and you allow your better nature to surface. You become naturally more powerful because you can no longer be manipulated or controlled by other people or adverse situations. Conversely, when your pride prompts you to fight, argue, or arrogantly resist a situation, your true self can never emerge, and you end up relinquishing your own power to others.

As tough as he looked, Daddy never once initiated a conflict himself. He was all about peacemaking, gentleness, and patience. There was something so pure about him; he was noble to his core. He was innocence and timeless wisdom wrapped up in one soul. After only a year, I already knew I had a very rare spirit walking by my side.

Daddy's puppyish insecurities rapidly gave way to a dignified self-reliance. Before he was even a fully grown adult, he

---

⭐ FROM THE CELEBRITY FILES

Whitney Cummings

Actor, stand-up comedian, writer, and producer Whitney Cummings credits many of the crucial lessons she has learned during her turbulent life to the wisdom of dogs — particularly, her own rescued pit bull, Ramona. "Having a pit bull teaches you about other people," she says. "When you see how people react to pits, you can tell a lot about the person. And you've also got that canine lie detector by your side."

Whitney believes Ramona has actually warned her away from some human relationships that could have been destructive. "She is my mirror," Whitney says. "She barks or gets anxious if I'm with the wrong guy." And Ramona, Whitney claims, always gets it right: "She knew if he'd been cheating, or was just a bad guy, period."

"We used to think 'humans are smart, dogs are not'—but that's so wrong," she continues. "Dogs are so much more connected and intuitive about what's going on. We get dismissive as we get older, and think we can only learn from those who are above us, but that's not true. You'll never know who you'll learn from today: a baby, a bumblebee, or a dog."

was well on his way to becoming a dog that the whole world would come to love and admire almost as much as I did.

A Member of the Pack

In the beginning, I was only hired to train and board Daddy for a few months. But those months quickly turned into years. Redman was in constant demand during the 1990s: Three of his successive albums went gold in the United States: *Dare Iz a Darkside* (1994), *Muddy Waters* (1996), and *Doc's da Name* (1999). After 2000, he began collaborating and touring with the artist Method Man; they even starred in a movie together. As a result, Red was almost never at home for long. Still, he and Daddy shared a genuine bond of love that never wavered. Whenever he was in town for a few days, I'd drop Daddy off at Red's house. The minute Daddy saw Redman, his tail would start wagging so hard that his whole body would wiggle. When Daddy and Redman reunited, they'd stay together for the few days Red had between gigs.

For the rest of the time, Daddy was a full-fledged member of my pack at the Dog Psychology Center. He was not a dominant dog, but he commanded instant respect and affection from the pack because of his gentle, nonthreatening manner.

Daddy was about three years old when I first noticed his "gift." When a new dog that seemed fearful or anxious came into the center, Daddy would go to its side and the dog would instantly begin to relax. If a dog came in with a chip on its shoulder and threatened the pack's stability, sometimes Daddy would step in and cool things down before I even got there. He had an inborn knowledge of how to manage any social situation, knowing how to show—with his energy and body language—that he meant no harm. But he also knew how to show other dogs when they were out of line. It was like he was saying to them, in dog language, "Chill. It's all good." I began observing his instinctual reactions and choices, and modeling the way I worked with dogs after Daddy's behavior. I found it made me even more effective at handling challenging canine cases.

The People Whisperer

Daddy wasn't just good at understanding dogs; he was uncanny at reading the character and core of people as well. I've always been intuitive about dogs, but I wanted to be able to have the same empathetic insight into my own species that he did.

By watching Daddy interact with people, I learned more about what makes them tick than any human could ever teach me. I used to bring Daddy with me to business meetings and watch how he reacted to the people in the room. Some people, he would shy away from or ignore. Others, he would approach politely, sniff, then roll over for a belly rub. Sometimes, Daddy's reactions would prompt me to either avoid or embrace a person or a situation. You could never hide your true intentions from Daddy.

Tolerance, Empathy, and Generosity of Spirit

During our 16 years together, Daddy taught me, step by step, each of the components that make up that rare and coveted quality called wisdom.

The first lesson was *tolerance*. One of the first traits of Daddy's that I noticed—even in his adolescence—was his extreme patience with smaller or younger dogs. There were two tiny Italian greyhounds, Lita and Rex, who lived with us at my Dog Psychology Center during those years. Inseparable little bundles of energy and mischief, they liked to clamber on top of Daddy, often curling around his body to go to sleep. He never complained.

Daddy also showed me that *empathy* for others is one of the vital cornerstones of wisdom. In today's world, when so many of us are caught up in competing, making a living, and struggling to take care of our family's needs, we often fail to see the greater struggle and suffering all around us.

Even as a puppy, Daddy was an incredibly keen observer of emotion, and was drawn to anyone—person or dog—who might be hurting. He was often one of the first to welcome a troubled new dog into the pack, and he instinctually gravitated toward the ones that needed his support the most. If a dog was feeling ostracized by the group, Daddy would become his welcoming committee and unofficial host. And if another pack member was feeling physically unwell, Daddy would offer his quiet comfort.

His empathy extended just as strongly to people. If someone in my family or on my staff was having a rough day or feeling sad, Daddy immediately sensed it. He'd go to them, plop his solid body down at their feet, and roll over on his back, inviting them to give him a "therapeutic" belly rub. When Daddy entered a room and sensed that someone was feeling down, he'd make a beeline for them, offering a nuzzle, a face lick, or a friendly tail wag of support. All my friends and colleagues who were fortunate enough to know him still

*Our fans adored Daddy and loved watching him work
with all of my cases on* Dog Whisperer.

talk today about how comforting it felt just to be around him. It was impossible to leave any encounter with Daddy not feeling uplifted and refreshed. It's like he was a born healer.

Daddy also taught me that *generosity of spirit* is another crucial hallmark of wisdom. There wasn't a person or an animal that he didn't greet with warmth and benevolence. While he was a flawless judge of character and intention, he never approached anyone with suspicion or hostility. He was very respectful and cautious, but always open-hearted. If he sensed someone didn't have his—or his pack's—best interests at heart, he'd casually move away from them.

Of course, if Daddy really cared about someone, there was nothing he wouldn't do for them. He was a giver through and through. Each morning, he liked to let my family or me know that he was awake by bringing us a gift: a shoe, a T-shirt, or

FROM THE SCIENCE FILES

Empathy in Dogs Is Real

Behavioral science has only recently begun to examine human empathy and cooperation. (For years, aggression and competition were deemed more important.) Since playing well with others has become a hallmark of what makes a civilization—or a species—successful, researchers now have turned to the question of whether or not dogs have empathy.

As it turns out, empathy in dogs (particularly toward humans) has a strong evolutionary advantage, and evidence for it has been found in dozens of recent scientific studies. The Royal Society's *Biology Letters* published an analysis of several studies on dogs and empathy through 2011.[8] The analysis established the following:

- Dogs react to their owner's stress with an increase in negative emotional arousal.
- Dogs "catch" human yawns. ("Contagious yawning" has been linked to elevated levels of empathy in humans.)
- When exposed to familiar people faking distress, dogs exhibit signs of emotional upset, strongly suggesting "sympathetic concern."
- Even untrained dogs are sensitive to human emergencies and sometimes act appropriately to summon help, which suggests empathic-perspective taking.

The study's authors stress the importance of continued research to measure and understand dogs' empathetic relationships with humans. After all, since more and more dogs are being employed to help us in dozens of new, therapeutic ways, we have a responsibility to safeguard their emotional well-being as much as our own.

a stuffed toy. He'd walk around with the item in his mouth, waiting for the subject of his generosity to notice. Then he'd fix his soulful green eyes on them, offer to let them take the toy out of his mouth, and end the ritual by walking away with his powerful tail erect and proudly wagging.

The *Real* Dog Whisperer

Daddy had been in my pack for about seven years when I started filming *Dog Whisperer* in 2004. I decided to bring him with me on cases right from the very beginning, and he proved to be quite a hit. Immediately, his popularity soared with audiences as possibly the best representative of the pit bull breed that the media had offered in a long time.

Daddy was the polar opposite of the "vicious" pit bull that is often stereotyped in the press. Anyone who saw the show immediately recognized him as more of a wise man or sha-man, assessing every problem situation and then showing others how it should be handled.

Like a spiritual teacher, Daddy had an endless supply of patience for the weaknesses and foolishness of others. He didn't have a mean bone in his body. He never bit any person or any dog—not even a nip. If they are pushed to the wall in self-defense, most dogs naturally use their teeth as their last resort—but I honestly don't think it ever would have occurred to Daddy to do so. Without fail, all it took was his calming presence and stoic dignity to de-escalate every situation.

I always refer to Daddy as an "ambassador for his breed," because although he looked tough, he could go anywhere and be comfortable with anyone. If there were conflicts in our family, Daddy would walk into the room and somehow diffuse the tension. If I was meeting someone for the first time and didn't know what to say, Daddy's huge head and body paired with his unexpectedly gentle demeanor were great conversation starters. Whatever situation I happened to be in, personal or professional, Daddy would arrive and somehow make it better.

Daddy appeared in many episodes of *Dog Whisperer;* his specialty was helping me rehabilitate the most aggressive and fearful dogs. Often, when I wasn't sure how to proceed with a case, I would call Daddy in and observe his behavior with the problematic dog. He would never create a fight or cause the other dog to flee. He would calmly assess the situation, then react appropriately. And whatever he did instinctually would inform the rehabilitation strategy I would choose for that dog. Of course, Daddy always got it right.

How Dogs Practice Wisdom

- Dogs are naturally open. Because they live in the present and are influenced only by what they are undergoing at any given moment, they always see every experience clearly and for what it actually is.

- Dogs are naturally empathetic. Through their sense of smell and their acute perception of energy, they can immediately tell what another animal is feeling or suffering—and it's in their nature to want to bring that animal back to a balanced state.

- Dogs are naturally communicative. Through their scent, energy, and body language, they say to each other—and to us, if we're paying attention—everything that ever needs to be said.

- Dogs are naturally observant. Their senses are far more powerful than ours, and they pay attention to everything in their environment. Thus, they are constantly processing information that we humans, with our self-centered worldview, often miss.

- Dogs are naturally authentic. When they love, they do so unconditionally, giving their hearts freely and forgiving liberally. As a result, they are able to see and appreciate only the best in other creatures.

Daddy and Cancer

When Daddy was around 10 years old, he came along with me when I visited a veterinarian friend who needed help with her dogs. Dr. Kathleen Downing must have noticed something subtle about Daddy that no one else had picked up on, because she told me I should bring him back for an exam. A week later, she found a mass in his prostate, did a biopsy, and sat me down with the terrible news: Daddy had cancer.

My first reaction was a feeling of confusion and helplessness. I make it a point to take the best possible care of all my dogs, but Daddy was always extra-special. When I called

Redman to tell him, he had the same reaction: "Why does this have to happen to such a beautiful dog?"

Dr. Downing told me there was a treatment protocol, but there was no guarantee that it would work. It would cost at least $15,000. Of course, I didn't hesitate to start the treatment immediately. As any dog owner knows, no price is too high for an animal you love.

I was by Daddy's side as he underwent a course of 10 two-hour sessions of chemotherapy. Blessedly, he handled the chemo really well; he had no vomiting or dizziness. Perhaps he slept a little more than usual. His stoicism astounded me. He never once showed any sign of discomfort, pain, or sadness. Perhaps he was withholding those feelings for my benefit. It's like he was saying to me, "Stop your worrying. What will be will be."

I did my best to follow his example and act as though everything was—and was going to be—fine. I shared his condition with only a few trusted friends and associates, because I didn't want people to project the negative and weak energies of sadness and pity onto Daddy's naturally upbeat outlook.

After Daddy underwent a final operation to remove his testicles, the doctor gave us the good news: He was cancer free. It wasn't long before he was back on the road with me for *Dog Whisperer*. And believe it or not, he seemed even wiser after the ordeal he'd so tolerantly endured.

Making It Official

For most of our years together, Daddy still officially belonged to Redman, even though he essentially lived with me full time. Because Red thought Daddy was the perfect dog—and he was!—he had always planned to breed him. That's why he never allowed me to get him neutered (though I would have preferred it, especially since Daddy would not have contracted prostate cancer if we'd had it done). We often forget how quickly time passes in dog years, and after Daddy had survived his cancer scare, I suddenly realized that he and I had been together for a whole decade.

Ultimately, Redman agreed to let me officially adopt his dog, even though he loved him very much. By that time, Daddy and I were inseparable, and Redman knew it was for the best. When we met to sign the adoption papers, that hard-bitten rapper from the mean streets of Newark, New Jersey, wasn't even ashamed to cry. He genuinely loved Daddy and continued to visit with him throughout the rest of his

At the Dog Psychology Center, Daddy (third from the right) was the one I relied on to integrate even the toughest dogs into the pack.

life. I'll always be grateful for Redman's selfless act in allowing me to adopt his dog. Daddy was our boy, and Red was ultimately at peace knowing that his dog would be staying with me. It was yet another example of Daddy's ability to elicit untapped wisdom and genuine, selfless love in the people he knew. Just like me, Redman found that being around Daddy made him want to act altruistically—even though it clearly hurt his heart to give his dog away for good. Sometimes, the most difficult decision is the right one.

"Pit bull Daddy is a bigger star than me," Redman told the A.V. Club blog in 2007.[9] "He's been on *Oprah!* If he stayed with me, he wouldn't have been the Daddy he's supposed to be. So I sacrificed letting my baby live with me, and he blew up! Now he's a star, man. That's another blessing."

> *When you get a dog, you inherit the dog's past and*
> *the wisdom of generations that the dog carries.*
> —Eckhart Tolle

Age and Wisdom

Daddy's wisdom grew with his age and experience. I remember that during one of the last seasons of *Dog Whisperer,* I was called in to help a very special Belgian Malinois named Viper, who was terrified of everybody. This was an elite dog specially trained to find hidden cell phones (and even the tiniest cell phone components) in jails; he was one of the most talented dogs to ever perform that very exclusive service.

At some point in his training, Viper had become afraid of the intimidating inmates whose cells he was required to search. That fear eventually morphed into a mistrust of all humans, to the point that he could no longer perform his job; Viper would either shut down completely or run away from any person he came into contact with. Since he had spent the first eight months of his life sleeping in a crate each night, he was reverting back to the experiences of his puppyhood. He just wanted to curl up in a safe space and hide away from the world.

Daddy and I went to see Viper and his trainer, who was desperate to get his valuable dog some help. We arrived at the building that had been designed as a "mock prison," specifically for training dogs like Viper to work in this unusual environment. I had Daddy wait outside in our *Dog Whisperer* mobile home while I went in to assess the situation.

When I arrived, Viper was already hiding under a table; I couldn't get him to come out. Food didn't work, nor did coaxing from his trainer. The camera crew was filming, and I was at a loss for what strategy to take. As I often did when I was stuck, I went to get Daddy's "advice." I opened the mobile home door, where he was waiting patiently.

Although he was about 15 years old, with arthritis and eyesight and bladder problems, Daddy didn't need me to tell him what to do, or even where to go. Despite the fact that he'd never even seen the building before, he trotted through the corridors and mock cells until he reached the room and the table under which Viper was hiding. Without missing a beat, Daddy ducked his achy old body under the table and touched Viper's nose with his own.

That was all it took. The dog came out, and Daddy demonstrated with his behavior toward me that I was a human he could trust. Daddy easily accomplished what neither I nor

FROM THE CELEBRITY FILES

Kathy Griffin

Comedian Kathy Griffin's offstage passion is rescuing dogs—especially hard-to-adopt senior animals. Kathy attributes her appreciation of the wisdom and insight that comes with age to her close relationship with her spry, witty 94-year-old mother.

"I have a joke in my act that I'm bored with anyone under 90, because the stories I get from my mom at 94 are unbelievable," she says. "In her, we have this sharp 94-year-old woman who's talking about the first time she ever met a gay person, the first time she ever heard about what civil rights were. This is a person who lived through world wars, and I just find that more interesting."

"I honestly think that is one of the reasons I actually prefer senior dogs," she continues. "I like the ones no one else wants, because they have this soulfulness you just don't find in puppies. I've had four that have lived to be at least eight. And I definitely saw them, as they aged, change in their behavior, just like people do. They become more accepting, and more mellow."

Viper's trainer could do. Thanks to Daddy, I was able to begin my work with Viper, gradually teaching him to trust humans again. After a few weeks' time, Viper was able to return to his work. With one touch of the nose, Daddy changed a dog's life.

There wasn't a single person on the *Dog Whisperer* crew who wasn't speechless that day. The Viper encounter was a clear example of Daddy's innate wisdom at work.

Respect Your Elders — Dog and Human

Daddy worked on the *Dog Whisperer* show into his extreme old age: the equivalent of 105 in human years. This made me happy, as I was raised to respect my elders. My grandfather's great wisdom—also gained after 105 years on this Earth— was venerated by all the people in his community, and especially by our family. I was reminded of that feeling by people's reaction to a white-muzzled Daddy. When they watched him limping into a house and helping a dog by calming it down or showing it a different way to behave, he shined a whole new light on what senior dogs can do.

The truth is, when you experience life with a senior dog, you are often getting the chance to spend time with one of the most perceptive, empathetic, and learned creatures on the planet. Across the board, my clients tell me that they believe their senior dogs "get it" and often make more soulful, fulfilling companions as they age.

I believe we should give even more to our senior dogs, because they have so much to give back to us. It's just another aspect of wisdom.

I have observed the aging process in many of the dogs I've loved in my life—but none more intimately than I did with Daddy. By the end of his life, we each knew what the other was feeling and thinking; we operated in a kind of "flow," where there was no effort, just unity. It was one of the most profound relationships I've ever experienced.

Of course I loved Daddy, but do I think Daddy loved me back?

I know he did.

Blessed is the person who has earned the love of an old dog.
— Sydney Jeanne Seward

Wisdom Never Dies

As Daddy got older, he became even calmer. Some dogs get smaller when they get older, but not Daddy. He only grew in stature and wisdom.

In our production offices, there was a special table for all the letters and packages that would arrive for Daddy from his fans all around the world—more, even, than arrived for me! There were thousands of requests for his picture and a pawprint "autograph," along with gifts of photos, homemade treats, and other handmade items. And above all, there were portraits: sketches, paintings, and even sculptures that people had been inspired to make of him. Among the funniest things we received were videos of other dogs watching Daddy on TV and getting excited every time he came on-screen. On more than one occasion, we were told that Catholic masses had been said for him. It was clear that the entire world knew he was truly something special.

What separated Daddy from the other wonderful dogs in my pack? You guessed it: wisdom. It made him a natural leader. Once, while we were filming in North Carolina, Daddy and I were invited to visit a V.A. hospital where veterans of the Gulf War—many of whom were amputees—

FROM THE SCIENCE FILES

The Chemistry of Love

"How do I know if my dog really loves me?" I hear this question from clients all the time. I always respond, "How do *you* know if *you* love someone?" Fortunately, science finally has given us a more satisfying answer.

Love is a crucial emotion for social animals — and in dogs, it's composed of the same chemical building blocks as the love shared between humans. In 2015, a Japanese study definitively linked dogs to oxytocin, the same "attachment hormone" that's shared between mothers and babies and that is also released when humans have sex.[10] When dogs stare devotedly into the eyes of their owners, their brains release elevated levels of oxytocin, strengthening the love bond between human and animal. The owners' brains, of course, reciprocate.

Effectively, this means that, neurochemically, a dog's love for her owner looks exactly like a mother's love for her baby or a husband's love for his wife. It also means we are capable of loving our dogs with the same intensity as we love our spouses and children.

Love is composed of more than chemicals, to be sure. But it's clear that a dog's love is "real" love, pure and simple. In the words of animal cognition researcher Dr. Brian Hare of Duke University, "When dogs are actually looking at you, they're essentially hugging you with their eyes."

were being treated. When we walked into a room, we could feel the respect these veterans had for Daddy, and I could sense the respect Daddy had for them.

I believe these soldiers saw Daddy as one of them: the ideal hero dog, big, strong, and noble. Daddy would puff up with excitement when they greeted him, and I think he felt proud that these human heroes were honoring him with their admiration. Every single soldier requested to meet Daddy and have a picture taken with him.

For me, the experience was different. I was touched and saddened by the sacrifices these men had made for their country. Many couldn't walk and were confined to wheelchairs. Some had lost friends and family on their return home. I wanted to ask how these men had become injured. I wanted to help. I brought feelings of sadness and inadequacy into the room with me.

But not Daddy. He could not have cared less about what had happened to these soldiers in the past. He didn't notice what was missing from their bodies or their lives. Daddy was simply happy to be in their presence. As always, he saw only their spirits, which were the spirits of heroes to him.

DADDY TOUCHED MILLIONS OF PEOPLE around the world. It's unfortunate that our fans in Asia and Europe never got to meet him in person, since I didn't start doing a lot of foreign travel until after his death. When I travel now, my fans the world over still ask me about him. They relate their favorite episodes and marvel at how profoundly he understood exactly how to help a dog and teach a human. Daddy taught his fans how to live.

Of course, one of Daddy's greatest achievements was the way he transformed the perception of pit bulls from being aggressive killers to peaceful, loving pets. My pit bull Junior continues to embody this message. Pit bulls are beautiful, gentle, patient, and intelligent dogs, and I will always have one by my side in order to convince the world that they've been wrongly victimized by ruthless humans. Thanks to Daddy, I think the message is finally getting through.

He taught us the art of unqualified love. How to give it, how to accept it. Where there is that, most other pieces fall into place.
—John Grogan, *Marley & Me*

Saying Goodbye

Daddy was strong and celebrated his life every single day— but Mother Nature will outmatch even the toughest among us. Though he'd had several great years after beating cancer, the telltale signs of age began to show when he turned 15 years old. Daddy had always wanted to join in the activities that used to be so easy for him—running with the pack, helping me on the TV series, stealing the show from me onstage at my live seminars. But little by little, physical activities became a strain for him. He had developed arthritis, and his hip joints were failing. Still, Daddy was a tough dog. Nearly blind and mostly deaf, he projected the same sage poise and nobility he always had.

Ultimately, his condition progressed to the point where he couldn't walk anymore. The final indignity was when he lost control of his bladder. I knew his time was drawing near as I watched the quality of the life he cherished diminish to the point where he had to spend most of his time lying on his bed, sleeping.

Daddy's tail would wag happily when someone he loved came to visit, and he always remained stoic and calm. But the vet told me he was probably in pain. While his tolerance for pain was enormous, I couldn't bear the thought of him facing any more suffering. I believe strongly that dogs will tell us when it's time for us to help them leave, and I understood that Daddy was telling me it was time for us to part ways.

The day that I made the wrenching decision to put him down, I called Redman and Jada Pinkett Smith to give them the news. They immediately came to my house to say goodbye, as did about a hundred of our other friends and neighbors. Everyone we knew had been touched by Daddy in some way.

When the news was made public, we received flowers and gifts from fans all over the world, even as far away as China, for weeks on end. Our house overflowed with so many arrangements and cards and stuffed animals that we could easily have opened a flower shop.

Daddy's life ended on February 19, 2010. He was 16 years old. The vet came to our house, which was quiet, serene, and dimly lit by candles (following a Mexican custom that honors the dying). When we were ready, the entire family gathered around Daddy. We said a prayer, and the vet administered a shot. Still praying, we watched the greatest dog in the world gently slip into his final sleep. Then I held him in my arms, weeping. My boys and my ex-wife were crying as well.

I am no stranger to death. On my grandfather's farm, I witnessed many, including those of some of the animals I'd cared for. Death was seen as a natural part of life. Then, when we moved to Mazatlán, I saw human death much more closely than a young boy ever should. In the mornings when I was walking to school, I'd often encounter people lying dead in the street after their adventures the night before.

Still, I didn't realize until the time came how unprepared I was to deal with the death of someone as close to me as Daddy was. In my heart, I wasn't ready—but I knew I couldn't be selfish. I understood on a gut level that it was Daddy's time, and I had to accept it.

That night, I thought about all we had been through together—working in the hood at the old Dog Psychology Center location, dealing with poverty, starting my TV show, traveling around America, overcoming cancer. Although I love my other dogs very much, I realized in that moment that there could never be another Daddy.

They say you can sometimes feel the spirit leave the body of a person when they die. But when Daddy passed, I felt something inside *me* leave forever.

Daddy's legacy did not die with him. From the day of his passing right up to now, I continue to receive packages containing original tributes and memories of him. I keep them in my home under a giant painting of Daddy created for me by Los Angeles artist Daniel Maltzman.

People watched *Dog Whisperer* because they wanted to see how Daddy was going to handle a tense situation. He gave hope to millions who were struggling with their dogs. Hope is what makes us strong. Daddy made me strong.

As I travel the world, I meet people in Asia and in other countries who are seeing *Dog Whisperer* for the first time. When they speak to me in person and learn that Daddy has passed on, they are shocked. Most of them will cry, even though they never met him.

I've never done a speaking engagement where I didn't talk about Daddy. When I do, I always tell my audiences, "I wish you could have met him."

I know beyond the shadow of a doubt that I would never have been as successful in my career without Daddy by my side, showing me the natural way to rehabilitate troubled dogs. I would not have been as dedicated a father without Daddy first showing me what unselfish love was like. I would never have become the man I am today without Daddy's otherworldly wisdom, inspiring me to treasure each moment, to remain calm, and to trust my instincts.

 ## DOG LESSON #6
How to Attain Wisdom

- ✅ Practice mindfulness. Use meditation, yoga, and time spent in nature as ways to silence the noise all around you. Eventually, your mind will clear and your intuition will improve.

- ✅ Cultivate compassion and empathy. Despite the fact that we live in a culture that rewards greed and selfishness, practice putting yourself in the place of others who are suffering. Then reach out and help them.

- ✅ Be present. Take a break from talking and thinking about yourself. Instead look and listen to what's going on around you. Observe without judging. Just stay quiet, take everything in and let it all be.

● Regard every experience in your life, good or bad, as a crucial lesson in your eternal classroom. There is a Buddhist saying that "when the student is ready, the teacher will appear." Always be aware that any person, animal, or event around you may become the "professor" you have always been looking for. Embrace their presence as an opportunity to take you to the next level of understanding.

LESSON 7:
RESILIENCE

*When you are deeply troubled, there are things you
get from the silent devoted companionship of a dog
that you can get from no other source.*
—Doris Day

Late in the summer of 2010, I was up at the Dog Psychology Center in Santa Clarita—just my pack and me. Something about the area reminds me of where I grew up in Mexico: the low, rolling hills; the scrubland; and the dry, high-desert heat. Two of Jada Pinkett Smith's huskies were pulling me on a sled I had modified to handle the bumpy terrain. My pit bull Junior and some of the other dogs ran alongside us as we navigated the trails and climbed the hills. I couldn't have felt more alive.

In that moment of pure joy, the hopelessness I had felt just a few months earlier was like a fading nightmare. I realized that I had been blaming all my dark feelings on the crushing and stressful events that were happening to me from the *outside*.

What I didn't understand was that in order to be free and to move forward in my life again, I had to heal from the *inside* first.

I said a prayer to give me clarity, and at that moment, I felt my life's mission blazing inside me, more strongly than it had in a very long time. I knew I still had a job to do—a special purpose on this Earth: to help dogs and to educate humans.

But I had a few outstanding issues to attend to first. After many months of grueling work, I finally concluded my divorce, severed all my unhealthy business relationships, and settled into a comfortable new home. And as the new direction of my life began to look more and more promising, my healing process could begin in earnest.

For this to happen, I decided to hit the reset button and to pull away from the work that had consumed me for so many years. Slowly, I began to reconnect with my true passions. I took a sabbatical from television and from my seminars, and centered my life on what had always mattered most to me: my dogs.

Over the course of nearly three months, I saw very few people except for close friends and family. Day after day, I sweated out my recent pain and resentments through heavy manual labor, painstakingly designing and re-landscaping the Dog Psychology Center with my own hands. Every other moment I spent with the dogs—walking, running, rollerblading, and playing with them.

I also made time to immerse myself in the activity that had inspired my lifetime passion for dogs in the first place: simply observing them playing and communicating so easily with one another. I sat quietly for hours, watching them interact. A thought ran through my head: Dogs always understand that life is simple. It's we humans who make it complicated.

As I watched them frolic along the slopes of the hillside—ecstatic just to feel the warm sun on their backs—I began to feel my own capacity for simple joy return.

During those many weeks I spent in near solitude, my pack gradually helped me restore my own ability to live fully in the present moment. Instead of dwelling on everything I thought I'd done wrong in the past, I began to feel grateful to be where I was, right then and there.

> *Dogs are often happier than men simply because*
> *the simplest things are the greatest things for them!*
> —Mehmet Murat Ildan, novelist and playwright

Disneyland

Nothing is more essential to resilience than being able to experience life the way dogs do, reveling in nature and living moment to moment. By this, I don't mean forgetting the past or ignoring the possible consequences of the future—not at all. But being fully present in our lives teaches us how to embrace the past and future in positive ways.

There's a saying they use in 12-step programs that has always resonated with me: "We will not regret the past, nor wish to close the door on it." The lessons of the past should not be forgotten, but they should not drag you down, either. If being in the moment reminds you of something in the past in a positive way, or it leads you to an idea that will help you improve in the future, you've got it right.

As my dogs towed me on that sled along the dusty landscape, I was filled to the brim with gratitude. I'd survived the painful aftermath of my divorce, and I was well on my way to healing and forgiveness. I was still painfully estranged from my sons—but somehow, feeling the strength and support of the pack all around me, I knew in my heart that we would all reconcile and be stronger than ever before. For now, I had my four-legged pack and a solid support system of family: my parents; my brother, Erick; and my sisters, Nora and Monica, as well as the many friends who had always stood by me through thick and thin.

Even though it was the steamy peak of summer, I felt like the character of George Bailey in the Christmas movie *It's a Wonderful Life*. At the end of the film, George's guardian angel, Clarence, leaves a special message for him: "No man is a failure who has friends." It's the moral of the film, and a

 FROM THE SCIENCE FILES

Linked by Our Genes?

Perhaps, as science seems to indicate, the human-dog bond goes even deeper than history and evolution. Perhaps it goes as deep as our genes.

In December 2005, a team of scientists announced in the journal *Nature* that they had sequenced the entire genome of the domestic dog.[11]

"Humans and dogs have the same gene set," says project leader, Kerstin Lindblad-Toh of Harvard's Broad Institute and the Massachusetts Institute of Technology. "In fact, every gene in the dog genome is the same as it is in the human genome, with similar function."[12]

good adage to remember in real life, too. Of course, if you have a dog, you always have a friend.

As my gratitude and zest for life began to return, my creativity and motivation began to bounce back as well. Watching my dogs play and noticing the different things that made them the happiest gave me a powerful inspiration. I thought to myself, "We say we love our dogs—but we usually engage them in activities that only make us humans happy. Why isn't there a place for dogs that focuses only on what makes the dogs *themselves* happy?"

Then it flashed before me: my vision for the future. I would turn the Dog Psychology Center into a Disneyland for dogs. I'd create a wonderland that would allow dogs to do what they love—swimming, hiking, carting, digging, agility courses, nose work, search-and-rescue exercises, and more. Then I'd add a menagerie of other animals to underscore a dog's place in the animal kingdom. I'd teach seminars for dog owners on how to fulfill their pets, so the owners, too, can create a joyful life for their pups. Then, as Walt Disney did, I'd spread the concept all over the world.

After a few months, when I finally felt ready to return to L.A. and get back to work, I discovered that my brother, Erick, had found offices for my new solo business in Burbank. The building looked like a fairy-tale Disney castle. I believed it was a serendipitous sign that I was on the right track.

When I told my small but loyal team about my "Disneyland for dogs" concept, they were all on board immediately, and we set to work. Before long, we made the Santa Clarita Dog Psychology Center all I'd imagined and more: a canine amusement park populated by dogs and a plethora of other animals—including horses, llamas, and turtles—with a huge swimming pool, an agility course, and a range of exciting activities for dogs. We made a small, hands-on seminar called "The Basics" available to owners so that they could learn to understand their dogs and fulfill their canine needs. Then, inspired by Disney, we headed to Florida and opened a second Dog Psychology Center—informally dubbed "Disneyland"—in Fort Lauderdale in 2014.

I'll always remember that landmark day in the high-desert hills above Santa Clarita when I recognized with joy that I'd really healed—spiritually, emotionally, and physically. And it was clear that dogs, and not human medicines, were responsible. Not only did they inspire me to call up the reserves of my own personal resilience and keep moving positively forward toward the future, but they also helped me without asking for anything in return. These four-legged angels saw me through my darkest spring and into the brightest season of my life.

Among the dogs in my pack that day at the center was my own special guardian angel: a brawny, three-year-old blue pit bull named Junior.

Dogs are wise. They crawl away into a quiet corner
and lick their wounds and do not rejoin the world
until they are whole once more.
—Agatha Christie

Raising Junior
Back in 2008, I was facing the painful reality that Daddy would not be with me forever. He had come through cancer

Jada Pinkett Smith

Jada has been one of my closest friends and confidants for more than 20 years. I first met her when I was still washing limos and training dogs on the side; she wanted to train her two Rottweilers to be personal pro-

tection dogs. We've been through thick and thin with each other, and her experience with the healing power of the pack perfectly mirrors my own.

"I'll tell you what my dogs did for me," Jada says one day while we're on a pack walk in the Santa Monica Mountains. "My dogs brought me back to my roots. I grew up in a war zone, in a neighborhood that was extremely dangerous. I grew up in a house without a father, I grew up in a house with a young mother, and I was prey. Every. Single. Day. When I was in the streets, I used to have this instinct, which was just survival."

But Jada says that once she began having success in Hollywood, that instinct started to dull, making her vulnerable. "You start to live in this protected bubble, you know?" she says. When she started working with me and learning how to handle a pack, she began to reconnect with her earlier self. "My dogs gave me a place where I could stay connected and keep those instinctual skills that I developed as a young girl on the streets of Baltimore sharpened—and be able to use them in a different way. Now I rely on those instincts to take care of business. I use them in deciding who I'm going to deal with and who I'm not going to deal with, and how I relate to people. My dogs brought me back to who I really am."

and rallied like a champ, but I couldn't deny that he was beginning to slow down. I knew that his extraordinary character would be rare to find in any animal. I decided he needed a protégé—an apprentice from the next generation to whom he could pass on his wisdom while he was still with us. I had a plan: Daddy would help me raise his ideal successor from puppyhood.

For Daddy Junior, as I would call him, choosing the type of dog was easy. Daddy had become the world's most beloved pit bull, and had helped countless hearts and minds to better understand his breed. I wanted another purebred pit by my side to continue the campaign of goodwill that Daddy and I had begun together.

Fortunately, a longtime friend whom I'd known since my days in Mexico called to tell me that he'd just bred his own gentle, submissive female pit with a beautiful purebred male who was also a calm, mellow show dog. He now had a litter of puppies that seemed to have inherited their parents' serene temperaments, and he wanted me to come see them. "Who knows?" he said. "You might find the next Daddy."

Daddy was riding shotgun in my jeep on the bright day I drove across town to meet the litter of six-week-old puppies for the first time. The squirming, clumsy little bundles of fur clambered all over us as I made quick evaluations from watching their behaviors with each other and with their mother: which one was the alpha, which was at the back of the pack, which were in the middle.

One pup immediately stood out from the rest. He was a velvety slate gray with a shock-white bib on his chest, and he had the most beguiling powder blue eyes. This type of dog is known as a blue pit (even though the blue eyes usually turn

It really was Daddy who picked Junior out of the litter, and he took on the role of mentor for that little pup from day one.

greenish or brown by the time the dog reaches adulthood). The puppy was adorable, but I wasn't drawn to his looks so much as I was to his energy. I got a chill as I picked him up. His mannerisms reminded me of a very young Daddy's.

Of course, since raising the puppy would primarily be Daddy's job, he should be the one to make the final selection. I gently picked up the pup and presented his rear end to Daddy, who sniffed it and indicated his interest. When I put the puppy on the ground, the little guy stumbled up to Daddy cautiously, holding his head down in a respectful, submissive way. I was impressed that a six-week-old pup was displaying such good canine manners already. When Daddy finished his examination of the puppy and turned to walk away, the little guy looked up, wagged its tail, and started to walk out after him! There was no mistaking it—we'd found our "Daddy Junior."

Junior was eight weeks old when we brought him home for the first time. From the very first night, he and Daddy were inseparable—sleeping together, eating together, playing together—with tiny Junior tottering along behind my creaky but still energetic sidekick, trying to emulate everything Daddy did. As soon as Junior had all his vaccines and it was medically safe, I started taking him everywhere with us. He accompanied me on speaking engagements and on pack outings to the mountains and the beach. I even started putting him in with the pack for *Dog Whisperer* episodes. When you're raising puppies, it's important to expose them to as many different kinds of situations as possible. The more adaptable your dog is, the more confident and balanced he will become.

 ## How Dogs Practice Resilience

- ✅ Dogs begin each day anew, so yesterday's worries, emotions, or concerns do not necessarily apply. Every day is an opportunity to start over; any failures, fears, or bad feelings from the past never last very long.

- ✅ Dogs tend not to display any kind of pain or injury, as appearing weak can be dangerous. This makes them more stoic—but also ensures that they bounce back quickly.

- ✅ Dogs are greatly influenced by their pack or the people around them—so if those in their social group are showing strength, even a timid dog will try to do the same.

✅ Dogs are curious and interested in new adventures, which helps keep them moving forward after a negative event.

Junior Grabs the Baton

In mid-2009, when Daddy was too weak to participate in many *Dog Whisperer* episodes, I began to ease in the two-and-a-half-year-old Junior as my right-hand dog, relying on him to help me with the unbalanced cases I tackled for the show. Because he'd spent his puppyhood following Daddy around and watching him closely, he knew right away what was expected of him (although I had to give him a lot of direction in the beginning). Today, at age seven, Junior is a beefy, beautiful bruiser in his prime, and his abilities have grown to the point that we share an unspoken communication—almost as strong as the kind I shared with Daddy.

In many respects, Junior is quite different from Daddy. Physically, he's taller and more tightly muscled; Daddy was stocky and had a thick, solid frame. And their personalities are very different as well. If life were a college yearbook, Daddy would be the mellow, thoughtful philosophy major, while Junior would be the happy-go-lucky jock. He's an able, agile athlete and a whiz with the ball—if I didn't set limits for his playtime, he could easily become obsessed with it.

What Junior can do with a simple baseball would blow your mind. He's also crazy about water, which isn't always the way with pits. Daddy was never a water dog; when I'd take the pack to the beach, he was content to watch from the shore and dig himself a special hole in the sand, but he didn't enjoy splashing after the ball in the waves like everyone else. Junior,

FROM THE CELEBRITY FILES

John O'Hurley

I'm not the first person whose dog has seen him through a rough divorce, and I'm certain I won't be the last. Best known for his role as J. Peterman on *Seinfeld,* the actor John O'Hurley told *Cesar's Way* magazine how his Maltese, Scoshi, saved him during his rocky post-breakup period.

"Scoshi and I took a long drive across the country, from New York to L.A.," he said in November 2010. "And we adjusted to the idea that our family had whittled down to the two of us. Dogs are so patient, and they just stay in the moment. They have no sense of past and future."

on the other hand, is such a proficient swimmer that he even swims underwater. He'll plummet down deep like a scuba diver, holding his breath with his eyes wide open, and pursue his ball if it happens to go beneath the surface.

A Shoulder to Laugh On

When I first moved out of the house I'd shared with my ex and my sons, I had to find myself a temporary single guy's apartment. The only dog I brought with me was Junior; the rest stayed with my staff at the Dog Psychology Center. We were two bachelors doing everything together—walking, commuting, eating, sleeping, watching TV on the couch. Even after I was on the mend, there were nights when dark thoughts would creep in and I'd be filled with loneliness, regret, and sorrow.

That's when I discovered another amazing quality about Junior: He is a natural entertainer, a clown. Junior always seems to know exactly when I need reassurance—and that's when he does something to crack me up. For instance, every morning this 70-pound pit bull acts like a comical puppy. He does a little dance, stretches out on the floor on his back, and looks at me to pull his paws up and rub his belly.

Junior is always game for some dog-on-dog silliness as well. He loves to play with our family pack, especially the smaller dogs like Coco, Benson, and Gio. He has a brawny, bar-rel-chested body, but when he plays with the little dogs, he'll try to tumble and act just like them—only he looks a whole lot clumsier. Watching him roll around trying to fit in with the tinier dogs never fails to make me laugh. He is not as agile and graceful as they are, but he seems to think he is!

When I was going through the worst hours of my dark journey, Junior saved my life. He made it impossible for me to stay angry or depressed for long. Though very different from Daddy, Junior was exactly the dog that I needed with me during that traumatic period. Of course, I had read all the research about the healing power of laughter, but I never really experienced it myself until I met him.

Resilience and Healing: Dogs as Therapists

Dogs have a special healing power that science is only now beginning to quantify and understand. It's not surprising to

FROM THE SCIENCE FILES

Do Dogs Have a Sense of Humor?

More than a century of research indicates that they do!

Charles Darwin was the first scientist to posit that dogs can have a sense of humor. In his 1872 book, *The Expression of Emotions in Man and Animals,* he describes the way some dogs will "tease" their master by "tricking" them into thinking they are retrieving a thrown object—but at the last minute, they'll pull it away and run away gleefully, as if playing a practical joke. Darwin viewed this as a behavior distinct from casual play.

Nobel Prize–winning Austrian ethologist Konrad Lorenz took things one step further by suggesting that dogs actually laugh. In his 1949 book *Man Meets Dog*, he wrote, "This 'laughing' is most often seen in dogs playing with an adored master. [They] become so excited that they soon start panting."

These same panting sounds that Lorenz observed as dog "laughter" were put to the test years later by Patricia Simonet of Sierra Nevada College in Lake Tahoe.[13] In 2001, she and her students recorded and analyzed sounds that were made mostly during play—and discovered that they were in fact quite distinct in pattern and frequency from

learn; I believe that millions of people have already been emotionally and psychologically healed by dogs. Throughout my life and career, I've watched dogs turn people's lives around where psychotherapy and medication had failed.

One of the most striking examples of this was the *Dog Whisperer* case of A. J., a client who had developed a serious ordinary dog panting. When Simonet played recordings of this dog laughter to young dogs and puppies, they responded with obvious joy, picking up a toy or posturing for playtime. Other recordings of various dog vocalizations, including ordinary panting, did not produce the same effect.

In 2009, the neuropsychologist and bestselling canine-behavior author Dr. Stanley Coren put Simonet's newly discovered "dog laughter" to more practical use.[14] He experimented with making the sounds himself until he'd perfected a workable human imitation of the pattern: "For me, what seems to work the best is something like 'hhuh-hhah-hhuh-hhah' ... This caused my own dogs to sit up and wag their tails or to approach me from across the room."

Coren next tried using those sounds to help soothe anxious dogs. He recorded positive results with all but the most severely anxious or traumatized cases. "This is reminiscent of trying to calm humans," Coren observes. "If they are moderately anxious, introducing some humor into the situation can be helpful and relaxing. But if they are in a state of panic, your attempts to lighten things up might be misinterpreted as belittling their emotional state and may actually make things worse."

Think about it: Do you laugh with your dog?

panic disorder akin to post-traumatic stress disorder after a long series of devastating personal losses and deaths in her life. Her anxiety was so severe that she feared going out in public, and spent most of her time hiding behind the walls of her house. But after she adopted a scruffy little terrier mutt named Sparky, she noticed she had fewer panic attacks—and when she did have one, she recovered much faster.

Sparky had helped A. J. where every other treatment had failed. He soothed her anxiety and quieted her fluttering heart. Just his presence in a room made her feel so much better. She decided to get him certified as a psychiatric service dog—a category of assistance animal that has only been recognized in the past 10 years—so he could go everywhere with her. The problem was that A. J. was deeply afraid of big dogs—especially pit bulls—and her fear had made Sparky aggressive toward the dogs that made her nervous. That was a problem because service dogs are not allowed to show any aggression.

I helped A. J. by bringing her to the Dog Psychology Center and surrounding her with more than a dozen friendly pit bulls who showed her so much love that she overcame her fears. And when A. J. stopped being afraid, Sparky's episodes

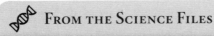 FROM THE SCIENCE FILES

Nature's Antidepressant

A recent study in the *Journal of Personality and Social Psychology* showed that pet owners were generally better off than non–pet owners, with lower levels of fearfulness and obsession.[15] Owners felt less depressed and lonely, experienced higher levels of self-esteem and happiness, and were less likely to feel stressed. Dogs seem to have natural antidepressant abilities and can do wonders for people's self-esteem, as well as reduce feelings of anxiety.

of aggression also vanished. A. J.'s experience was transformative, and with a better-behaved and certified Sparky by her side, she emerged from her cocoon stronger and more together than ever before.

Eight years later, A. J. has improved both her mental and physical health and is now one of Los Angeles' most sought-after vegan chefs. Brimming with life and confidence, she attributes her new life to the healing power of one little dog.

I personally wish more psychiatrists today would scribble "rescue a dog" on their little white pads before prescribing medication.

Recently I received an email from a fan with a rescue-dog success story that is a beautiful testament to the power of healing and resilience. I've left out names and identifying details out of respect for the sender's privacy:

Dear Cesar:

I have battled with depression since high school and it hasn't been easy. Medications, therapy, anxiety, more medications. It's been almost 20 years of on and off; some times are good, some really bad. Life changes aren't as easy for me as for most people. Some things can cause a bout of depression that may seem endless.

In 2012, I adopted my odd husky mix, who was a day away from being put down after being rescued from the side of a road. Since the day her foster parents opened their door and let her run to me, life hasn't been the same. I cried with joy to see that beautiful face, her green eyes filled with such happiness and gratitude for just being there. Since that day, she has helped me deal with my depression, and has given me a reason to get up in the morning and do the things most people can without a second thought.

When all I want to do is lie in my bed and sleep, my dog is there looking at me with those eyebrows and an expression of "let's play." I get up, give her a great big hug, tell her how much I love her, and that I couldn't do without her. She has turned my life around.

Just knowing she was only three weeks old and almost put to death makes me look at things very differently now.

Except in the case of natural disasters, severe early-life trauma, organic brain damage, or inbreeding issues, dogs themselves don't experience mental health issues unless they're caused by humans. We are the ones who make them crazy and unbalanced. Dogs can develop issues and phobias from unstable humans or stressful environments in which they're not getting their own needs met. But once removed from those negative situations, they often recover completely (thus my observation that "dogs will always go toward balance"). What's remarkable is that they have the power to bring us back to balance, too.

NINE WAYS DOGS IMPROVE OUR MENTAL HEALTH

1. They offer us the calming effect of physical touch.

2. They provide affection and raise our self-esteem.

3. They reduce our isolation and lone- liness.

4. They encourage empathy by giving us responsibility for another creature.

5. They help us build new human relationships.

6. They distract us from negative thoughts and feelings.

7. They encourage us to maintain healthy routines like exercising and keep us on simple schedules.

8. They raise our serotonin levels when we're with them.

9. They provide us with the healing power of laughter.[16]

One compelling example of how a dog's outlook can improve a human's mental health and foster resilience is the case of Owen Howkins, who we first met through *Cesar's Way* magazine in August 2012. Owen was born with a rare genetic disease called Schwartz-Jampel syndrome, which means his muscles are always tensed. His childhood was painful. He realized from the time he was a very young boy that people would look at him differently, and he became increasingly self-conscious about his appearance—marked by dwarfism, a smallish head, and abnormally small eyes. Like A. J., Owen withdrew into his own world, clinging more and more to the safety and isolation of his house.

At the same time, an Anatolian shepherd called Haatchi was also suffering. He was only 10 months old when someone tied him to a railroad track and left him to die. A train

Owen Howkins and his three-legged dog Haatchi are the perfect pair.
They build each other's confidence and approach life with no judgment.

took off one of his hind legs but, miraculously, the dog managed to escape with his life. He lay bleeding and whimpering, all alone by the tracks for days, until he was rescued by Owen's dad, Will, who brought the three-legged dog home to his family.

I've worked with many three-legged dogs in my life, and all of them act as if there is nothing missing from their bodies. Amazingly, most have been able to keep up with the pack on morning hikes. And the dogs they interact with don't care that their companions are missing a limb, or an eye, or part of a tail. Dogs just don't view each other with that kind of judgment, and Haatchi didn't look at Owen as if he were different either.

When Owen first looked into Haatchi's loving brown eyes, his life changed in an instant. His new pet's unquestioning acceptance of his condition gave the boy the confidence to venture outside his home again. Owen cared for Haatchi, taking him on walks and bringing him to dog shows; as a result, he was filled with a new sense of purpose and self-confidence. Owen has also lost his fear of strangers—because with Haatchi around, he now has something to talk about.

Therapy Dogs

Hospitals are filled with pain, fear, and sadness, and I can think of few places where dogs are more desperately needed.

Outside of a war zone, hospitals are considered one of the most stressful places for humans to be. Filled with a distinctive set of smells, many hospitals betray the same

 From the Celebrity Files

Dr. Andrew Weil

Dr. Weil, an integrative medicine practitioner, says he's actually "prescribed" dogs for patients as part of therapy. In 2012, he told *Cesar's Way* magazine that "having a dog is enormously beneficial to emotional well-being." A dog relies on you to meet its needs, which "prevents you from becoming too focused on yourself, which is not healthy."

Weil continues, "My two Rhodesian ridgebacks remind me that spontaneous happiness is a real possibility, because they demonstrate it in front of me every day."

Bringing Hospitals Into the 21st Century

David Frei, author of *Angel on a Leash: Therapy Dogs and the Lives They Touch,* is the voice of the Westminster Kennel Club dog shows. His wife, Cherilyn, is the Catholic chaplain at Ronald McDonald House in Manhattan; together, they have been passionate advocates for getting more therapy dogs into hospitals.

"A lot of people in health care didn't want dogs in the hospital when we started," David says. "But now, science is catching up with what dog owners have always known."

David visits hospitalized children with his two Brittany spaniels every week. "When a dog walks in the room, the energy changes. Patients talk when they haven't been talking, smile when they haven't been smiling. Dogs live in the moment, and they give these patients a moment."

combination of bodily fluids, medications, cleaning solutions, and rubber, making them very unpleasant places. And despite the goal of silence and serenity, most are filled with constant background noise: hushed voices, moans and coughing, the hiss of respirators, the beep of monitors, telephones, loudspeaker pages, and elevators dinging.

Thanks to their energy, compassion, and heightened senses, therapy dogs that visit and comfort patients have proven to be just about the best medicine a hospital can offer. The best hospital-visit dogs are the happy-go-lucky ones from the middle of the pack. They are friendly and curious to just about everyone, and bring positive energy with them. All the smells humans dislike provide a vivid palette for the canine nose, but dogs don't attach negativity to them. They also don't come in weighed down by guilt, pity, or worry.

As everyone knows, hospitals house people at their weakest. Dogs bring optimism, hope, curiosity, and joy—all the qualities that a sick or injured person desperately needs. A good therapy dog will enter a room and immediately go straight to the sickest or most emotionally needy person there. She'll then continue around the room until all the patients are projecting the same positive energy. For dogs, the energy of pain and illness becomes something to be corrected, and bringing the room back to balance poses an interesting challenge.

I trained Junior as a therapy dog and had him officially certified in 2012. This, in essence, is his role on my series *Cesar 911* (but on the show, the therapy he provides is primarily for other dogs, not for people). Junior proudly wears his official "Therapy Dog" vest, which allows him to travel with me anywhere; people can look at him and feel confident he's well behaved, calm, and highly trained. When he's got his vest on, people also know he's working and is not to be petted or distracted.

The art of healing comes from nature, not from the physician.
Therefore the physician must start from nature,
with an open mind.
—Paracelsus

Paging Dr. Dog, Oncologist

No reflection on the many dimensions of resilience would be complete without examining dogs' miraculous ability to not only facilitate physical healing but also to help catch diseases before it's too late. Case in point: cancer-sniffing dogs.

The discrimination in a detection dog's sense of smell is quite remarkable. These special animals are tasked with spotting a needle in a haystack, over and over again. But due to the fact that they possess approximately 100,000 more smell receptors than we do, detection dogs are able to recognize the distinctive scent of the cancer cells and their waste products — sometimes, even when the cancer has barely taken hold. Dogs are also able to identify chemical traces of a substance in a human body in the range of parts per trillion.[17] And they know when there's a smell that shouldn't be there.

Today, detection dogs can smell and recognize cancer long before laboratory tests detect it, with a remarkable accuracy rate of 98 percent.[18] Catching the disease at this early stage — including some of the deadliest varieties of it — means transforming it from fatal to curable.

At long last, science has finally caught up with what our dogs have been trying to tell us for thousands of years. We've only just begun to teach them how to communicate their valuable knowledge to us.

In the spring of 2010, I was fortunate enough to be able to visit one of these remarkable detection training centers. At the Pine Street Clinic in San Anselmo, California, head trainer Kirk Turner explained how he was able to teach a dog to detect cancer in just two and a half weeks. He did so using baby food containers or empty film canisters containing the cells and/or urine from a person with the disease, with holes poked in the lids so the scent can come through. The dogs would be given several containers, and were trained to sit down next to the container that contained the target scent—in this case, cancer cells. A correct answer earned that dog a reward—a treat, affection and praise, or a play session—depending on that dog's individual preference.

Michael McCulloch, the director of the clinic, told me of the time a dog-in-training once detected a cancer relapse in a woman whose own doctors wouldn't find the new tumor for another year and a half. She was part of the control group that provided breath samples from people who were supposed to be cancer free. Twenty-four out of the 25 times dogs sniffed her sample, they indicated cancer by sitting down in front of the sample and not moving. When this woman's doctors found the new tumor, it was still so small that it was barely detectable; it was literally at what they called "stage zero." Her doctors were able to remove it completely.

Another amazing story involved a startling incident that happened at a highly competitive dog show. One of the participants being judged for his beauty had a side job that the organizers didn't know about: He was one of the first schnauzers to become a cancer-detection dog. But there was a hitch: One of the rules of the show is that the dog has to remain standing during the judging, or risk disqualification.

When the cancer-sniffing schnauzer drew near to one of the judges, the dog immediately sat down and wouldn't move. Of course, he was immediately disqualified. But before leaving the ring, the schnauzer's handler took the judge aside and advised her to get checked by her doctor.

A few days later, the judge called the handler to thank him. She told him that her doctors had discovered stage II breast cancer. If not for the dog, she probably wouldn't have found out in time to be successfully treated.

Of course, the dog didn't care that he was disqualified from the show. He had done what he was trained to do—save people's lives.

Diabetes-Alert Dogs

I was at a dressy cocktail reception recently when something made me look up. In walked a magnificent golden retriever wearing a service vest and backpack, commanding everyone's attention. The gorgeous animal was accompanying a woman in her 30s, and the two of us talked for a while.

Technically, the Americans With Disabilities Act prohibits strangers from asking a handler what her disability is (and it's also a little impolite). But the young woman recognized me right away, offering up the fact that she was a type 1 diabetic, that her dog's name was Hardy, and that he'd been with her for three years. The dog not only alerted her to dangerous fluctuations in her blood sugar levels; he also carried her insulin in a medical kit and other emergency supplies in his backpack. Diabetic-alert dogs detect blood sugar changes through the breath of their handler. They're also explicitly trained to seek outside help should their human ever pass out or become incapacitated.

The woman removed a red plastic collapsible water bowl that was clipped to the side of Hardy's backpack. "It's just smart to bring him with me to events where I might accidentally eat something that could send me out of balance without knowing it," she told me, pouring a plastic cup of water into the bowl and putting it on the floor. "And not only that: I never have to worry when I don't know anybody in the room. People always approach us, and there is always something to talk about."

Sofia and Monty

Sofia Ramirez adopted Monty, her long-haired miniature dachshund, when she was in the market for a potential show

 FROM THE SCIENCE FILES

How Dogs Heal Us

- Diabetic-assist dogs detect and alert type 1 diabetics when their sugar is too low.
- Seizure-alert dogs warn their owners when an episode is coming on, so they can take their medication or get to a safe place.
- Assistance dogs help the blind, deaf, brain-injured, or chronically ill (for example, those who suffer from Parkinson's disease). They are trained to perform daily tasks, guide their handler in public, and alert both the handler and others to potential life-threatening conditions.
- Psychiatric-assistance dogs aid those with mental health issues by providing comfort and physical touch.
- Therapy dogs bring joy to nursing homes and hospitals.
- Allergy-alert dogs detect potentially deadly allergens in food or in the environment.

dog. But soon afterward, when she was diagnosed with hypoglycemia, she noticed that Monty would react strangely whenever she had a fainting spell or developed a headache. Sofia eventually made the connection and realized that her new pet would make an excellent service dog.

After extensive training, Monty began to help keep an eye on Sofia's blood sugar level. If it begins to drop, Monty will paw Sofia and alert her to take her medication. "I use a meter, but it's easier to forget to use it than it is to forget a dog trying to get your attention," she explains. "If it weren't for Monty, I probably wouldn't be here right now."

The remarkable thing about Monty is that he demonstrated this ability on his own, before he even embarked on training. He only needed to be taught what to do when Sofia's blood sugar dropped. So many of the ways dogs benefit human health seem to come directly from their inborn, natural abilities.

The dog's most important job is still around.
Like the legendary Cerberus, the dog still keeps
many of us from the Hell of Loneliness.
—Tara and Kathy Darling, *In Praise of Dogs*

TBI and PTSD Service Dogs

Since the beginning of the conflict in Iraq and Afghanistan, soldiers have been coming home with a unique cocktail of afflictions. First, a traumatic brain injury (TBI) is often the aftereffect of improvised explosive devices. A TBI is an injury that you can't see but that affects a person's frontal lobe and can lead to diminished capacity in everyday things that the sufferer used to take for granted. Seizures or fainting spells can happen to TBI victims, and the injury also has a profound influence on personality and can result in subtle or extreme changes in memory, emotional affect, and temperament. Although it's an actual physical injury, it's inside the brain and can't be seen. That's why a TBI's side effects are demonstrated most clearly in a person's postwar behavior.

The second signature injury of the war on terror is post-traumatic stress disorder (PTSD). This is another injury you can't see that is a serious mental health disorder. Its symptoms can be horrifying: flashbacks, nightmares, and unwanted traumatic thoughts, as well as extreme fear, anxiety, mistrust of others, guilt, loneliness, and the inability to feel pleasure. Because PTSD also affects personality, sufferers can become isolated as friends and family members struggle to understand their loved one's strange new behaviors. Isolation leads to loneliness, and loneliness leads to severe depression. Since the war on terror began, the U.S. military and Department of Veterans Affairs have both documented an epidemic of PTSD-related suicides.

Enter a new breed of American heroes: PTSD and TBI service dogs. These animals are individually trained to help each veteran or active-duty military member with his or her particular form of PTSD or TBI. The dogs can learn hundreds of different personally tailored tasks, including summoning assistance in a medical crisis, warning of a seizure or panic attack before it happens, or providing such treatment-related assistance as carrying medications and offering touch therapy. These dogs also assist the patient in coping with emotional overload by offering a soothing presence and performing security enhancement tasks like preventing other people from crowding or overwhelming the patient.

Veterans Affairs already provides service dogs to physically injured veterans and has just begun to issue PTSD-trained dogs to troop members diagnosed with that affliction. The dogs are providing invaluable help in integrating traumatized veterans back into the civilian world. Since this is a new area of therapy-dog work, the hard data and statistics are still coming in. But the anecdotal evidence from the servicemen and -women themselves firmly supports the concept of PTSD dogs for veterans.

While anecdotes connecting dogs and resilience have been reported for thousands of years, there's now ample science to back it up. I personally believe that a dog will always be the best medicine in the world.

Resilience and Unconditional Love

I believe I understand dogs better than I understand people—and I sometimes believe dogs are the only ones who truly understand me. Being around a pack of dogs brings me the kind of serenity I can't find anywhere else. I am an old-fashioned guy who believes in honor and tradition, and I observe these qualities much more often in dog communities than in human ones. The values that dog packs operate on—loyalty, authenticity, and mutual support—are harder to come by in modern society.

My relationship with Junior is only just beginning to approach the deep intimacy of my relationship with Daddy.

I have always sought the same kind of loving relationship with humans, but could never quite find it.

That is until, I met my Jahira.

After all the papers for my divorce were signed and I was officially a single man, I went through a period of self-doubt and insecurity. I was worried about my business and my sons, and I was feeling rejected and unlovable. One day in 2011, while I was doing some retail therapy at Dolce & Gabbana in Los Angeles, I saw a stunningly beautiful woman working there. TV show or not, I just knew a woman like that would never go out with me. So I put my head down and walked past her to the elevator that led to the men's section.

Right before the door closed, that gorgeous young woman got into the elevator with me! I've never known what to say in situations like this, but she made the conversation easy. She told me that her name was Jahira and she was a stylist who had only been in Los Angeles a few months. When I introduced myself, she said she liked my TV show. After a short exchange, we parted ways, but I couldn't get her out of my mind. I especially liked her admission that she was proud as a young Latina to have her job in a very prestigious store. Her confidence made an impression on me. I few weeks later, I mustered my nerve and came to the store again—this time, not to shop, but to ask Jahira to dinner. That's how it all began.

We dated for some time and, as we grew closer and closer, talked about living together. Meanwhile, while his brother Andre remained with his mother, my youngest son, Calvin— then 10 years old—had decided to come live with me. No longer just a divorced, "weekend dad" in Calvin's life, I was grateful to once again be able to be with him every day—but at the time, he was a handful. The divorce had made him—as it had me—unsure of himself and his place in the universe. He was angry, having trouble at school, and doing a lot of rebelling.

When Jahira finally did move in, she immediately took on a very maternal role with Calvin. I watched as she set a warm and loving example for him. And gradually, with her unflinching support, Calvin's anger subsided.

We were two broken men, and Jahira—young but incredibly wise for her years—knew just how to put our pieces back together. She gave us unconditional love at the lowest point in both our lives and challenged us to be our best. She believed in us even before we believed in ourselves again. And miraculously, we both managed to rise to the occasion.

I have never experienced a love like the one I share with Jahira.
She has been a bright spot in my life.

Jahira was the woman who finally taught me to trust people. My relationships with my dogs—particularly Daddy—had always been very deep and satisfying. These relationships were based on authenticity and integrity; I never had to be anything but myself for them to love, respect, and treasure me. But I had never felt completely comfortable with the humans in my life. I realize now that I always had a wall up.

Jahira was the person who dared me to tear down that wall. She taught me that when there is mutual trust between two people, it's possible to form the deepest and most precious of human bonds.

I have never before experienced the kind of unspoken connection that Jahira and I share with each other. So often one of us will start a sentence and the other will say, "I was thinking the same thing." Or I'll remember something I need to do, and she'll turn to me and say, "Don't worry, babe. I already took care of it."

Jahira has the most generous heart I've ever known. The way we interact is filled with the same high level of respect and honor I have experienced with the animals who share my life. I never thought I could experience this kind of unconditional love and trust with a human, but Jahira makes it easy. And it feels wonderful.

That's why I've asked Jahira to marry me.

It took a lot of years and a lot of dogs to help me heal. Dogs were the inspiration for my resilience: They showed me how to free my heart up to have an unconditionally loving relationship with one human. But as I've always said, old dogs do learn new tricks. And even this old dog can change at any time.

DOG LESSON #7
How to Be Resilient

- ✅ Connect to calm energy. It reduces stress that can lead to mental and physical illness. You will also benefit from lower cortisol levels and blood pressure.

- ✅ Exercise to heal inner wounds. Develop a regular routine and choose the low-intensity activities that dogs do: walking, swimming, and running.

- ✅ Face up to your problems. Being in denial only prolongs the healing process.

- ✅ Accept yourself without judgment, and don't focus on the perceived judgments of others. If you accept yourself, others will follow suit.

LESSON 8:
ACCEPTANCE

*Accept—then act. Whatever the present moment
contains, accept it as if you had chosen it ...
This will miraculously change your whole life.*
—Eckhart Tolle

Just the other morning, I opened up the *Los Angeles Times* to read this welcome headline: "No Charges for 'Dog Whisperer' Cesar Millan After Animal Cruelty Investigation."

This official statement from Los Angeles County Animal Care and Control came a few months after its 2016 investigation into my dog rehabilitation techniques.

Dogs are constantly revealing new and valuable life lessons, and this incredibly disheartening episode became another one of those teaching moments. The cruelty charges against me offered the opportunity to take a crash course in advanced spiritual acceptance—and my unlikely teacher turned out to be the dog at the center of the incident: a tiny black-and-white French bulldog named Simon.

Let's go back to the beginning.

Simon and the Pig

On my television series *Cesar 911,* people call our production offices to report cases of problem dogs that need to be fixed immediately. Often, there is a crisis looming: a marriage at stake, a possible eviction, or even—as in the case of Simon— the possibility that an out-of-control dog may have to be put down.

Like all the dogs that are featured on my show, Simon had a compelling backstory and an urgent problem. It all began with a call from Jody and Sue, both members of a breed-specific rescue group called Pei People, which rescues—you guessed it—Chinese shar-peis. Like many rescue groups, the organization finds most of its dogs in high-kill shelters and places them in foster care while the rescuers search for their forever homes. In their foster homes, the dogs have a chance to heal from neglect, abuse, injury, or disease.

Simon's owner, Sandy, was one of Pei People's best volunteer foster moms. She would take on even the sickest, most injured, most extreme rescue cases. Over the years, she had taken in more than 60 shar-peis and nursed them back to health until they could find loving homes. I greatly admire people like Sandy, who open their homes to animals in need. They are truly angels in disguise.

The problems began when Sandy adopted a pet of her own: Simon, a French bulldog with an overload of attitude. Although he was a loving pet to Sandy, Simon, from the time she took him in, gradually grew more and more aggressive toward the dogs his new owner was fostering. Eventually, his potential aggression became a real danger.

Sandy already had two beloved pets at home when she adopted Simon: a pair of potbellied pigs. One day when she was out, Simon brutally attacked them. He killed one on the spot. The other was so badly injured it had to be euthanized. Sandy was traumatized and devastated by the incident.

When they called me, the Simon situation had come to a head. Sandy and the Pei People were in a very bad place. The rescue group had come to depend on Sandy to take their toughest cases, but feared it would be too dangerous to send her any more dogs while Simon was in the house. Now Sandy was facing a "Sophie's choice" of her own: either retire from rescuing the dozens of homeless shar-peis that needed her unique form of help, or euthanize Simon, who was far too aggressive to give away.

I have said, and I'll say again, that I do not believe in euthanizing dogs for the majority of behavior issues. In my experience, only a small percentage of problem dogs can't be helped by the right humans—and even then, they don't deserve to die for it (especially when 99 percent of the time, humans created those problems in the first place).

Simon Accepts the New World Order

When I'm called in to help someone who rescues or fosters dogs, I know that I have a big responsibility. It's not just that one person or dog I'm helping—it's countless other dogs who will be helped by that rescuer. Once I met Simon and observed his aggression toward Sunshine, the shar-pei that Sandy was fostering, I knew he was a serious "red zone" dog. The "red zone" means that if left unchecked, the animal's aggression can escalate to the point where some might actually kill, leading to tragedies like the sad fate of Sandy's potbellied pigs.

The first part of my work was teaching Sandy how to de-escalate Simon's behavior toward her foster dogs before another tragedy took place. Simon was a challenging case, and I definitely earned my living working with him that day. Still, I eventually found that, like most dogs, Simon was open and receptive to having new limits set on his behavior. It was just that no one had ever given him any limits before.

I spent a very long day working with Simon until he became amenable to a whole new way of interacting. While the full process of his rehabilitation would take much longer (including a stay at the Dog Psychology Center that we scheduled for the following week), Simon showed a remarkable willingness to change. Like most dogs, he naturally preferred harmony to conflict; he just had never been shown

What the audience didn't see from one short clip was that exposing Simon to pigs helped him overcome his aggression toward other animals.

another way. In fact, when I finished at Sandy's house around sunset, I was gratified to see the feisty little Frenchie chilling comfortably on the front porch, right next to both Sandy and another dog, Sunshine.

Dogs surrender to change so beautifully. Like so many of the dogs I work with, Simon needed only a day to begin accepting the new structure at his home.

I couldn't have known then that, soon, I would be the one who'd have to face my own struggle with acceptance and surrender.

Acceptance of what has happened is the first step to overcoming the consequences of any misfortune.
—William James

Simon Faces His Demons

Since dogs much more readily accept change than we humans do, I believe it's important for them to face whatever they fear or dislike, so they can accept a completely new way of interacting with the world. If a dog is compulsive about chasing squirrels, he has to be around squirrels so I can train him not to act out in a predatory way. In the past, I've helped dozens of dogs this way by bringing in the object of the dog's fear or aggression and, with repetition and clear boundaries, teaching them to form new and positive associations.

My approach with Simon was no different. When I learned that he had attacked pigs in the past, I called my producer, Todd Henderson, and asked him to track down some pigs. I grew up with pigs in Mexico, so they are very familiar to me.

Chances are that sooner or later, some will probably join my merry menagerie of horses, goats, llamas, chickens, and tortoises, all coexisting happily and peaceably at the Santa Clarita Dog Psychology Center.

Simon stayed with us at the Dog Psychology Center for two weeks, during which time I exposed him to any and all animals that might become objects of his aggression—goats, pigs, horses, and, of course, other dogs. By the time he returned home to Sandy, he was eating, playing, and walking—with not only the pigs but also all the animals and dogs at my ranch.

 ## How Dogs Practice Acceptance

- Dogs are among nature's most successful species, since they are biologically wired to adjust to changes in their environment and circumstances.

- Dogs have the ability to accept circumstances that humans would consider traumatic—living in new climates, responding to new human-given "names," and adjusting to new and different packs—more easily than their owners can.

- Dogs are easily able to accept limits if they are offered with calm, assertive energy.

- Dogs accept aging, illness, and disability (like the loss of a limb or blindness) gracefully and adjust with minimal trauma.

● Dogs experience deep emotions like grief at the loss of a fellow animal or human, but they always move on.

● Dogs living among each other often choose surrender over conflict in order to live peaceably. This is the foundation of acceptance.

One 20-Second Clip

Sandy, Pei People, my team, and I all considered Simon's rehabilitation an unqualified success. That's why the tempest that followed was such a shock to me. It became a true test of my own ability to roll with life's punches.

In March 2016, the National Geographic Channel's social media team released a promotional video for an episode of the show in which Simon's story was to appear. Unfortunately, the promo was a 20-second, out-of-context clip in which Simon—still in the very beginning stages of his rehab—attacks a pig, nips its ear, and draws blood.

Looking back, that video seemed far too sensational, without any of Simon's backstory or what was at stake for him and Sandy. If they'd watched the entire segment, viewers would have realized that by the time Simon met the pigs, he had already undergone some heavy-duty rehabilitation. They'd also have seen me put Simon on a leash to see how he would react to the pigs. It was only after he showed no signs of aggression or interest in the pigs that I removed it.

Despite the dramatic editing of the promo that made the attack look bloody and violent, audiences of the complete episode would have learned that the veterinarian's report on the pig read "minor scratches." And finally, they'd have seen the happy ending: Just 15 minutes after the altercation, Simon and the pig were walking peacefully together down the road.

But in 20 seconds, viewers couldn't know any of that. Only a few days after the promo aired, my team learned that a petition was already being circulated around the Internet, denouncing me for "animal cruelty." I was accused of "baiting" a dog with a pig. Someone was even upset that the owner of the pigs grabbed one by the back legs to keep it from running away. (Anyone who, like me, has grown up on a farm will tell you that when you need to stop a pig from running, that's pretty much the best way to do it. If the pig had bolted, it could have incited an even more aggressive attack from the nearby pack of dogs.)

It didn't matter that the early critics got all their facts wrong. The media smelled blood and big ratings before anyone had even called my team for a comment.

This was one of the hardest lessons in acceptance I have ever faced.

For the duration of my career in the public eye, I've had a mass of appreciative friends, fans, and colleagues who support what I am trying to do with dogs, and who understand the genuine motivation behind the work. At the same time, there has also been a very vocal group of critics—made up of both the public and some professionals—who have loudly disagreed with my approach to dog rehabilitation (or rather, what they often wrongly believe my "techniques" to be).

As it happens, very few of these people have ever reached out to me personally to share their criticisms in a constructive way. Those who have are usually surprised that I am always open to listen to their ideas. By the end of these conversations, we tend to discover that they disagree with the *words* I use—for example, "dominance" and "assertiveness"—to describe my methods, but not necessarily with the methods themselves. In addition, while many of these critics train and condition dogs that have ordinary pet dog problems, they have never faced a long-term struggle to rehabilitate a red-zone dog whose very life is at stake.

I don't hide what I do—it's all on tape, and it's all out there on TV. There have been public criticisms of me—sound bites spoken, op-eds penned. I am used to it. I understand that most of these people are genuinely concerned with the welfare and health of dogs and other animals, and believe, rightly or wrongly, that they are doing something to help. If someone whose work or opinion I respect makes a clear, constructive suggestion for me, then I always pay attention. The rest—the white noise of negativity—I've learned to disregard.

All of us must learn to accept discord. Needing the whole world to love and agree with you in order to feel good about yourself is not a realistic goal. I have one way of doing things, but that doesn't mean there can't be many other ways that are just as good. Disagreeing is part of our culture—now, more than ever. Politicians don't agree with other politicians (even with those on their own side). Scientists don't agree with other scientists. Doctors don't agree with other doctors. Dr. Phil is not for everybody; Dr. Oz is not for everybody; Oprah is not for everybody.

I disagree with people, too. I disagree with my children. I disagree with my family members. I disagree with people in the media. But what I have trouble accepting is hostile close-mindedness in the words and actions of a tiny percentage of people who mischaracterize what I do. In the case of Simon and the pig, they didn't even know most of the facts of the situation. But once they made up their minds, they instantly saw me as the wrongdoer.

I also saw how easy it is for one unproven accusation to nearly topple a mission that took two decades to build. I was a working father; for more than 10 years, I sacrificed a lot of time away from my kids because I really believed that I was helping people better understand their dogs. That was and still is my life's purpose. But for me to continue my work, people have to trust me.

It takes a long time to build trust, loyalty, and respect. It takes a long time to build a career and a life's mission. Tragically, it takes only seconds for a misguided human throwing around loaded words like "animal cruelty" to threaten to tear it all down.

> *Reflect upon your present blessings—*
> *of which every man has many—and not on your*
> *past misfortunes, of which all men have some.*
> —Charles Dickens

Surrender Conquers Anger

Indirectly, Simon the French bulldog had forced me to rise to another challenge. Would I, like Simon, be able to accept what was happening, no matter the outcome? Or would it cause me to become as bitter and angry as my accusers? This tough but ultimately successful case was now putting my understanding of the concept of surrender and acceptance to the ultimate test.

One important way I coped with the onslaught of what felt like hatred being directed toward me was by never taking these accusations personally. My critics don't know me as a person; they aren't my friends; they don't know my heart or soul. They don't know the deep love I feel for the animals in my life or the profound communication that passes between my dogs and me when the cameras aren't rolling. People who don't know me can't hurt my essential self.

And that's what I learned from dogs: They may scuffle and confront one another, but once that conflict is done, they immediately move forward again. They never hold a grudge. So instead of hitting back, I took a page from what I have learned from dogs and held on to my faith that something positive would come out of all this angst.

As a Mexican man growing up poor, with no trust that the government (or sometimes, even my parents) could help me when times were tough, I learned to hold on to something bigger. For me, that something was God. Whether or not you believe in God, the universe, Uncle Sam, or the Flying Spaghetti Monster, acceptance means having faith; a faith strong enough to get you through. Faith that—in the face of hate, negativity, or even losing everything you have—will guide you to the other side of your troubles a better, stronger, and wiser person than you were before.

As difficult as it was to persevere during those weeks of investigation, I chose acceptance and faith as the right courses to take. My team and I opened ourselves up fully to the investigation and let justice take its course. The authorities watched the episode in question—reviewing it many times—as the whole story unfolded, captured on two different cameras. They researched and discovered for themselves the precautions we had taken for both the dog and the pigs before filming began. Shortly after the incident occurred, they were able to see the same pig running happily through our yard with no sign of trauma to its ear.

The inspectors came to the Dog Psychology Center and evaluated our facilities and our practices; then they took statements from the key people involved. When they read the full report written by the veterinarian who tended to the pig immediately after the attack, they saw that his only criticism of our safety practices was that we should probably have used stronger sunscreen on the pigs, because it was such a hot and sunny day.

The outcome was the public exoneration I read about in the newspaper: "After a comprehensive investigation by our officers, we presented a very thorough and complete report to the District Attorney's office and they were unable to find anything to charge Mr. Millan with,' said Aaron Reyes, deputy director for animal care and control. 'It's a fair decision.'"[19]

Of course, I was confident that any investigation into my Dog Psychology Center and our top-notch *Cesar 911* production team would result in exoneration, since we had done nothing wrong. We had nothing to hide. Furthermore, we were honestly engaged in an all-out effort to rehabilitate and actually *save the life* of a dog in need. The authorities later admitted to our team that they regretted the whole incident, which had wasted valuable time, city resources, and manpower. Nevertheless, being unjustly accused of animal cruelty was possibly the most traumatic professional experience I've ever had.

Think about it: What is the worst thing you can say of a person who has devoted his entire life to helping animals? Just whisper that terrible word "cruelty." It's a word that

 FROM THE SCIENCE FILES

Self-Acceptance May Be the Key to Happiness

The University of Hertfordshire in England, in coordination with the charities Action for Happiness and Do Something Different, surveyed and rated 5,000 people through questions that determined their place on the 10-question Happiness Scale.[20] The questions were based on the latest scientific research on what makes happy people different from unhappy ones. One startling discovery was that self-acceptance was the quality that most correlated with happiness, but it was the least frequently practiced. On a scale of 1 to 10, nearly half (46 percent) of respondents rated themselves below a level 5 in self-acceptance.

The study recommended the following habits to boost self-worth and self-acceptance:

- Be as kind to yourself as you are to others. See your mistakes as opportunities to learn. Notice things you do well, however small.
- Ask a trusted friend or colleague to tell you what your strengths are or what they value about you.
- Spend some regular quiet time by yourself. Tune in to how you're feeling inside and try to be at peace with who you really are.

conjures up images of negativity, hate, and violence—the polar opposite of my work with dogs.

I try to look at every experience in my life as a lesson, and sometimes, those lessons are hard-earned. So is the lesson of *acceptance*.

Rehabilitating the Ego

Acceptance is a lesson we all struggle with. Unlike other animals, we human beings are burdened with the weight of our self-esteem, which we call ego. Our egos can be positive—they inspire us to create, to imagine, and to reach for goals that may seem impossible. But its darker side is its ability to override our intellects—and especially, our instincts. Ego's voices chant that we are the center of the universe, that we deserve to be on top, totally fulfilled and happy 100 percent of the time. Most dangerous of all, it allows us to think that we can control everything in our lives and in our worlds.

Acceptance is the ability to silence the ego's constant rumblings and to recognize that there are some things in life we absolutely cannot control: death, nature, and especially the thoughts, feelings, and actions of other people. Acceptance allows us to sit back, take a deep breath, and let things be when a situation is beyond our ability to handle. In "Dog Whisperer" terms, the ego has to be *rehabilitated* for us to find peace in uncertainty.

I've always been interested in spiritual growth and in trying to be a better person, so I've worked on mastering acceptance for a very long time. In some areas, I feel that I've conquered it. When I work with dogs, I accept them as they are and don't judge them for their past or current actions. I don't become angry even if they try to attack me, and I don't work against Mother Nature. I believe my job is to help dogs get back to the core of what they are meant to be: animals first, then breeds, then their human-given names.

My clients with problem dogs often confuse the order of their pets' identities — usually by thinking of a dog as his name first, then as his breed, and then all too frequently, considering them as human! They tend to forget that even though our dogs are undoubtedly members of our families, *Canis familiaris* is in fact a very different species from our own. Dogs have different needs and desires, and we must learn to fulfill them to keep our pets happy and in balance.

In teaching my clients this lesson, I actually become a teacher of acceptance. So you'd think it would be easy to transfer that ability into my own dealings with the human world, right?

Wrong! I admit that I find humans puzzling and complex. For me, acceptance of their often contradictory thoughts and actions is much more difficult than simply allowing a dog to be a dog. But if there is one thing that I know about humans, it's that I'm not alone in my frustration.

That's why I believe acceptance is one of the most important lessons our dogs can teach us.

The brilliance of dogs is that since they don't possess our egos, they can't reference our detailed but malleable memories. They don't make up stories about the past that reinforce their own denial; they don't hold grudges, and they can make new associations far more easily than we can, leaving all remnants of their pasts behind. Simon is a great example of how dogs achieve this.

★ FROM THE CELEBRITY FILES

Kathy Griffin

As a standup comedian, Kathy Griffin has faced ruthless competitors, half-empty houses, and drunken hecklers. When she comes home from her workday of running the showbiz gauntlet, she looks to center herself. She achieves this with her family of rescue dogs: Chance, Captain, Larry, and Pom Pom.

"They are not judging me," she says. "I just watch them, and they make me laugh because they are so honest with each other. I strive for that in my humor because it's that rawness that the audience responds to. In a metaphoric way, my dogs are the opposite of some of the celebrities I joke about. They don't try to be anyone but who they are, and they love you unconditionally for who you are."

More Happy Endings

Simon the French bulldog taught me the most difficult lesson of my career: the ability to accept that people can hurt and even try to destroy something they fear or don't understand. I now can pass this lesson on to my kids. We have to accept that this dark side of human nature exists before we can learn to rise above it.

It's important to remember that between the two of us at the center of this incident, Simon had far more at stake than I ever did. If I'd failed to rehabilitate him, he would have paid for my failure with his life, condemned to death and euthanized for being a hopeless case.

Today, many months after we filmed the episode, Simon's dramatic attitude change is only growing stronger. His aggression has receded, and he can now coexist safely in the company of pigs, dogs, and a variety of other animals. Sandy is still fostering rescued shar-peis, and she's even adopted her foster dog Sunshine permanently, because he and Simon—once a dog who hated other dogs—have formed an inseparable bond!

Now *that* is the beautiful outcome I'd hoped for.

Once again, it takes a dog to teach us how acceptance can bring about a new, more balanced, and peaceful way to live.

 ## Dog Lesson #8
How to Practice Acceptance

- Observe your circumstances and consider the events and behaviors that brought you to where you are with an open mind.

- Don't repeat the same behavior if you keep getting negative results.

- When offered a new and better way to behave or to live, don't fight it; open yourself up to embracing it.

- Always strive to move toward balance, not conflict.

- Have faith in something larger than yourself—whether it be your pack leader, your family, your life's mission, Mother Nature, or your God.

EPILOGUE

Dogs are loyal, patient, fearless, forgiving, and capable of pure love. Virtues that few people get through life without abandoning, at least once.
—M. K. Clinton, *The Returns*

J ust before finishing this book, I returned from my second major journey to Asia, to teach people about dogs. The first time I went there, in 2014, I did only my seminar tour. This time, I not only gave more seminars in Hong Kong, mainland China, Thailand, and Singapore; I also filmed a new television series called *Cesar's Recruit,* a contest-style reality show where I work with ordinary people who want to become dog trainers to discover my next apprentice—and who might one day be known as the Asian "Dog Whisperer."

The many differences between Eastern and Western cultures are fascinating for me—a kid from a Third World country—to observe. And as it happens, Asian audiences actually seem far more receptive to the kind of calm, assertive leadership that I teach than American and European audiences are. For thousands of years, Asian culture has always featured restraint, discipline, loyalty, calmness, and respect as its core values. Although most people who attend my seminars there have had very little education about how to care for and connect with their pet dogs, they tend to pick up immediately on what I have to say, in a much more comprehensive way than some of my Western audiences do.

The responses I've received from my work in Asia have been astounding. Dog owners there report remarkable results after my seminars, by just applying their age-old cultural values to their relationships with their pets. As a result, I returned to the United States filled with great optimism about the future for dogs in Asia, where dog ownership among the middle class is a relatively new phenomenon, but where people are clearly eager for positive information on how to care for and fulfill their new four-legged friends.

While many Asian societies still use dogs as food, I still believe that Eastern cultures are perhaps a perfect fit for those who love and appreciate dogs as friends, helpers, and companions. Certain ancient Eastern religions believe God put dogs on this Earth to teach and guide us. Others believe that when an especially sagacious and worthy person dies, his or her soul's final incarnation on Earth will be as a dog, since they are the wisest and most enlightened of earthly beings. Given all the life lessons I've learned from dogs, I don't think it's such a far-fetched thing to believe. Perhaps the ancients of the Asian world intuited something about the canine soul that longtime dog-loving Western societies are just now beginning to understand?

To be followed home by a stray dog is a sign of impending wealth.
— Chinese proverb

I have learned much from the most important people in my life. My grandfather taught me respect; my mother taught me unconditional love; my sons taught me patience and restraint; my fiancée, Jahira, taught me trust. But I can say without hesitation that it was my relationships and interactions with the dogs in my life that made every one of those lessons come alive to me. Dozens of other dogs from my past have shown me wisdom that no human could have: A delicate Doberman pinscher called Baby Girl taught me about perseverance as I worked for months to help her overcome the most debilitating case of fear I've ever seen. Gavin, a bomb-sniffing dog from Afghanistan with PTSD, taught me what it means to be a true, selfless hero. Apollo, my son Andre's Rottweiler, taught me about the healing power of play and gentle energy. Without Daddy and Junior to show me the meaning of loyalty and unconditional love, I would never have been able to become the steadfast father and romantic partner that I've finally become. Dogs taught me how to go after my dreams, how to fall in and out of love, how to bear disappointment, how to weather loss, how to laugh with abandon, and how to move on and forgive.

Going all the way back to my childhood with Paloma on my grandfather's farm, dogs also gave me my inspiration and mission in life, as well as the confidence and courage to carry my message to the rest of the world. I'm infinitely blessed to get to work with dogs every day of my life, because that means the lessons just keep on coming.

I'm lucky to be surrounded by dogs like Junior.
The dogs that I work with teach me new lessons every day.

And that's a good thing, because I believe I have a lot more learning to do. A human brain is more complicated than a dog's brain, and the human ego—well, sometimes, I think overcoming that is just about the biggest challenge God has ever put in front of us. Like all humans, I am a work in progress.

Learning from dogs has hardly made me perfect. Ask me if I have had any bad relationships—intimate or otherwise—and the answer is yes, absolutely. Have I turned out to be the perfect parent? No. Did I raise perfect children? No. But ask me if I've ever raised a perfect dog, and I'll tell you yes, many times. That's because dogs begin life in the perfection of simplicity—and if we just allow them a safe and structured place to fulfill who they are inside, their character will take care of itself.

We humans lack dogs' inborn capacity to be guileless and innocent—and only the most enlightened and spiritual among us will ever experience the purity of living completely in the moment. But even if we can't emulate dogs completely, we can welcome the best qualities of their pure and beautiful spirits into our lives. The happiness, freedom, and simplicity that a true connection with a dog—or dogs—brings are surely some of life's most precious gifts.

> *Dogs are how people would be if the important stuff*
> *was all that mattered to us.*
> —Ashly Lorenzana, author

So now, close your eyes one more time. Imagine with me your day ends like this:

> *You return home from a fulfilling day's work with a spring in your step. The moment you enter your home, you and your loved ones reunite as if you haven't seen each other in years— you embrace, dance, sing, and celebrate—affirming and reaffirming your appreciation of and unconditional love for one another. After some vigorous outdoor recreation and a belly full of dinner, you all lie quietly together on the lawn and marvel at the night smells, the crickets' songs, the flickering stars. Nobody speaks, yet so much is communicated. Nothing more needs to be said.*
>
> *Later, you all fall asleep in one another's arms, exhausted and grateful, without any worry or doubt that the next day won't be as magically joyful as the one you have just finished.*

Your last sentiment before sleep envelops you is a feeling of thankfulness that you are blessed to live such a rich and gratifying life.

These simple but profound lessons that dogs can teach us are much too important to ignore.

We just need to pay attention to them.

Now go out and—to paraphrase a popular saying—dare to be the person your dogs think you are!

Sources

1. Marc Bekoff and Jessica Pierce, "The Ethical Dog," *Scientific American*, March 1, 2010, www.scientificamerican.com /article/the-ethical-dog.

2. Allen R. McConnell et al., "Friends With Benefits: On the Positive Consequences of Pet Ownership," *Journal of Personality and Social Psychology* 101, no. 6 (December 2011): 1239–52.

3. Sophie Susannah Hall, Nancy R. Gee, and Daniel Simon Mills, "Children Reading to Dogs: A Systematic Review of Literature," *PLoS One*, February 22, 2016.

4. Leanne ten Brinke, Dayna Stimson, and Dana R. Carney, "Some Evidence for Unconscious Lie Detection," *Psychological Science* 25, no. 5 (May 1, 2014): 1098–1105.

5. Jeffrey T. Hancock et al., "On Lying and Being Lied To: A Linguistic Analysis of Deception in Computer-Mediated Communication," *Discourse Processes* 45, no. 1 (2007): 1–23, DOI: 10.1080/01638530701739181.

6. Akiko Takaoka, et al., "Do Dogs Follow Behavioral Cues From an Unreliable Human?" *Animal Cognition* 18, no. 2 (March 2015): 475–83.

7. K. A. Lawler, et al., "The Unique Effects of Forgiveness on Health: An Exploration of Pathways," *Journal of Behavioral Medicine* 28, no. 2 (April 2005), 157–67.

8. Karine Silve and Liliana de Sousa, "'Canis Empathicus'? A Proposal on Dogs' Capacity to Empathize With Humans," *Biology Letters* 7, no. 4 (2011): 489–92, DOI: 10.1098 /rsbl.2011.0083.

9. Nathan Rabin, "Redman," *A.V. Club*, April 10, 2007.

10. Miho Nagasawa, et al., "Oxytocin-Gaze Positive Loop and the Coevolution of Human-Dog Bonds," *Science* 358, no. 6232 (April 17, 2015): 333–36.

11. Kerstin Lindblad-Toh et al., "Genome Sequence, Comparative Analysis and Haplotype Structure of the Domestic Dog," *Nature* 438, no. 7069 (December 8, 2005): 803–819.

12. Quoted in Scott P. Edwards, "Man's Best Friend: Genes Connect Dogs and Humans," *BrainWork* (blog), DANA Foundation, March 2006, www.dana.org/Publications /Brainwork/Details.aspx?id=43592.

13. P. Simonet, M. Murphy, and A. Lance, "Laughing Dog: Vocalizations of Domestic Dogs During Play Encounters," *Animal Behavior Society Conference*, July 14–18, Corvallis, Oregon.

14. Stanley Coren, "Do Dogs Laugh?" *Psychology Today*, November 22, 2009.

15. J. M. Siegel, "Stressful Life Events and Use of Physician Services Among the Elderly: The Moderating Role of Pet Ownership," *Journal of Personality and Social Psychology* 58, no. 6 (1990): 1081–86.

16. The health benefits in this list are described in more detail in Michele L. Morrison, "Health Benefits of Animal-Assisted Interventions," *Complementary Health Practice Review* 12, no. 1 (January 2007): 51–62.

17. Tamanna Khare, "Can Dogs Sniff Out Cancer?" *Dogs Naturally Magazine*, www.dogsnaturallymagazine.com /can-dogs-sniff-out-cancer.

18. G. Taverna, et al., "Prostate Cancer Urine Detection Through Highly-Trained Dogs' Olfactory System: A Real Clinical Opportunity," *Journal of Urology* 191, no. 4 (2014): e546.

19. Sarah Parvini, "No Charges for 'Dog Whisperer' Cesar Millan After Animal Cruelty Investigation," *Los Angeles Times*, April 11, 2016.

20. University of Hertfordshire, "Self-Acceptance Could Be the Key to a Happier Life, Yet It's the Happy Habit Many People Practice Least," *Science Daily*, March 7 2014, www.sciencedaily.com/releases/2014/03/140307111016.htm.

Resources

Further Reading
Animals Make Us Human: Creating the Best Life for Animals
By Temple Grandin and Catherine Johnson
Houghton-Mifflin Harcourt, 2009

Are We Smart Enough to Know How Smart Animals Are?
By Frans de Waal
W.W. Norton and Company, 2016

Beyond Words: What Animals Think and Feel
By Carl Safina
Henry Holt and Company, 2015

The Emotional Lives of Animals: A Leading Scientist Explores Animal Joy, Sorrow, and Empathy—and Why They Matter
By Marc Bekoff
New World Library, 2007

The Genius of Dogs: How Dogs Are Smarter Than You Think
By Brian Hare and Vanessa Woods
Dutton, 2013

How Dogs Love Us: A Neuroscientist and His Adopted Dog Decode the Canine Brain
By Gregory Berns
Harvest, 2013

How to Speak Dog: Mastering the Art of Dog-Human Communication
By Stanley Coren
Free Press, 2000

Inside of a Dog: What Dogs See, Smell, and Know
By Alexandra Horowitz
Scribner, 2009

Rewilding Our Hearts: Building Pathways of Compassion and Coexistence
By Marc Bekoff
New World Library, 2014

When Elephants Weep: The Emotional Lives of Animals
By Jeffrey Moussaieff Masson and Susan McCarthy
Delacorte Press, 1995

Wild Justice: The Moral Lives of Animals
By Marc Bekoff and Jessica Pierce
University of Chicago Press, 2009

Organizations

Cesar's Way
www.cesarsway.com
Cesar Millan's online home

Cesar Millan's Mutt-i-grees Program
www.education.muttigrees.org
Guided by research on resiliency, social and emotional learning, and human-animal interaction, the nonprofit Mutt-i-grees curriculum includes lesson plans and strategies to actively engage students and promote social and emotional competence, academic achievement, and awareness of the needs of shelter pets.

Cesar Millan PACK Project: People in Action for Canines and Kindness
www.millanpackproject.org
A nonprofit organization dedicated to improving the lives of dogs by reducing euthanasia, overpopulation, and suffering, while also educating humans to build respectful, healthy relationships with dogs. Together we will create a better world for us all.

Dognition: Discovering the Genius in Your Dog
www.dognition.com
Citizen science research project by Dr. Brian Hare of Duke University and other scientists, which includes games to play and exercises to uncover the unique way your dog thinks, feels, and solves problems.

ACKNOWLEDGMENTS

Cesar Millan

My deepest love and gratitude to the woman who won my heart and supports me in everything I do, Jahira Dar. Thanks to Bob Aniello for getting this book off the ground and for your consistent wise counsel in work and in life, and to Melissa Jo Peltier for bringing your talents and dedication back to our team. To my sons Andre and Calvin Millan, thank you for teaching me every day how to be a better father and for making me so proud of you both. Thanks always to my friend Jada Pinkett Smith, who has stood by me through so much. And finally, thanks to Daddy, my guardian spirit, whose extraordinary life and soul inspired me to put these memories, feelings, and ideas into words.

Melissa Jo Peltier

Thanks to Bob Aniello and Jon Bastian at Primal Intelligence for the thorough groundwork you laid for this book. To Hilary Black at National Geographic Books, thanks for your dedication, diligence, patience, and perfectionism. A shout-out to my crack legal team, Shaliz Shadig, Domenic Romano, and Miles Carlsen, and to my friend Carolyn Doyle Winter for your smart critique and editorial work. To Kay and Murray Sumner, thanks for your warm friendship and hospitality during the writing process. Many thanks, of course, to Cesar Millan—it was so nice to work with you again after such a long time. Eternal gratitude and love to the man who always has my back, my husband, John Gray. And to my four-legged muse and "writing partner" Frannie, I'll thank you later with an off-leash romp by the Hudson.

ABOUT THE AUTHORS

Cesar Millan
Star of Nat Geo WILD's *Dog Whisperer With Cesar Millan, Cesar 911,* and *Dog Nation,* Cesar Millan is the most sought after dog behaviorist in the world. He is the author of the *New York Times* bestseller *Cesar's Way* as well as *Be the Pack Leader, A Member of the Family, How to Raise the Perfect Dog,* and *Cesar Millan's Short Guide to a Happy Dog.* He is the founder of the Dog Psychology Center, based in Santa Clarita, California. In addition to his educational seminars and work with unstable dogs, Cesar has founded Cesar's Way and the Cesar Millan PACK Project, a nonprofit organization dedicated to animal rescue, rehabilitation, and rehoming. He lives in Santa Clarita with his pack of six dogs and his fiancée, Jahira.

Melissa Jo Peltier
Melissa Jo Peltier was co-executive producer of the Emmy-nominated National Geographic WILD series

Dog Whisperer With Cesar Millan, as well as Mr. Millan's co-author for five previous *New York Times* bestsellers and three other nonfiction titles. She is also an Emmy-winning veteran television and film writer, director, and producer with over 50 other national and international awards to her name. Her first novel about the entertainment business, *Reality Boulevard,* was named by *Kirkus Reviews* as one of its "Best Indies of 2013." Peltier lives in New York with her husband and their rescue pit mix, Frannie.

ILLUSTRATIONS CREDITS

Now Available in Paperback!

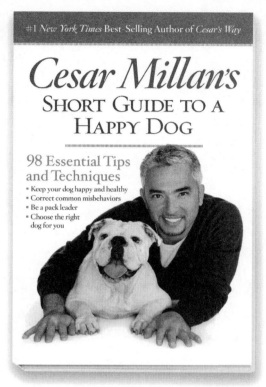

#1 *New York Times* Best-Selling Author of *Cesar's Way*

Cesar Millan's
SHORT GUIDE TO A HAPPY DOG

98 Essential Tips and Techniques

- Keep your dog happy and healthy
- Correct common misbehaviors
- Be a pack leader
- Choose the right dog for you

"[Cesar is] serene and mesmerizing . . .
He deserves a cape and a mask."
—*New York Times*

From the world's most celebrated dog behaviorist and *New York Times* best-selling author, this practical, easy-to-follow guide will help you build a happier, healthier relationship with your canine companion.